£1.20

The Pan Book of Winemaking

D1394294

The Pan Book of
WINEMAKING

B.C.A.Turner
Past President, National Association of Amateur Winemakers

revised edition
Pan Books London and Sydney

First published 1964 as *Improve Your Winemaking* by
Pelham Books Ltd
Published 1965 as *The Pan Book of Winemaking* and
reprinted five times
This revised edition published 1976 by Pan Books Ltd
Cavaye Place, London SW10 9PG
2nd printing 1978
© B. C. A. Turner 1964, 1976
ISBN 0 330 24770 0
Printed and bound in Great Britain by
Richard Clay (The Chaucer Press) Ltd, Bungay, Suffolk

Contents

List of illustrations

'Son, they have no wine.'
Gospel according to St John, II, 3

Preface to the second edition

Since it was written this book has been reprinted many times and used all over the world to produce good wine. With the advent of the metric system, the opportunity has been taken to revise the text completely and to introduce the latest techniques. To facilitate finding them quickly, the specific gravity tables and the tables of weights and measures have been placed at the end of the book. In addition to the list of mail order suppliers given in the Appendix, ingredients can be bought from your local Boots the Chemist and your nearest Home Brew Shop of which there is at least one in most towns.

The number of new wine- and beer-makers increases day by day and the quality of their wine improves steadily with their knowledge and experience. This revised edition of a very popular book will help you to improve the quality of your wine.

B.C.A.T. 1975

Acknowledgement

It is with sincere gratitude that I
acknowledge the intelligence, skill and
tenacity of my wife, who prepared the
typescript from an illegible manuscript.

Information in this book was
correct at the time of going to press

Regimen sanitatis

Dis ist ein Regiment der gesuntheit durch
alle Monadt des gantzen Jares/wie
man sich halte sol mit essen vnd
auch mit trincken vñ saget
auch von aderlassen.

1 Why make wine at home?

The Portuguese have a saying to the effect that some knowledge of wine is a sign of education, and without doubt one of the best ways to acquire some knowledge of wine is to make it.

The earliest written record of winemaking is about 2100 BC, but it is certain that wine was known and made long before then. Throughout the centuries and all over the world, men and women have fermented the local juices of one kind or another to make a drink that gladdens the spirit and adds life and vitality to the company. In this country we are blessed with an abundance of innumerable fruits, flowers, vegetables, cereals, herbs, shoots and trees from which palatable and potent drinks can be fermented. Many of these fruits and flowers grow wild in the hedgerows and meadows and as a result the cost of a bottle of good, honest wine indigenous to the neighbourhood need be little more than the cost of the sugar.

Here, then, is perhaps one of the strongest motives for making wine at home. When everyday wine in the shop costs so much, a comparable one – to say the least – can be made at home for a tenth of the price. With the cost of so many good things in life so high from taxation and labour, here is one source of gracious living for almost nothing. The housewife searching for something 'different' for a blasé family can transform her 'same-ish' meals into repasts that are remem-

bered because she has readily to hand a wide variety of
wines with which to cook.

Tough joints can be marinaded till tender, cheap fish can
be exalted in the company of wine, sauces can become exotic
and fresh fruit will develop flavours that recall the great days
before modern mediocrity. And withal, there is always a
glass of wine with the meal and another later to carry the
blessing of relaxation to its proper conclusion.

Today more than ever before, we need to drink wine every
day to combat the stress and pace of our daily lives. Wine
relaxes tense nerves, raises up the heart and dissolves inhibi-
tions. The daily tonic stimulates the appetite drugged by
cigarette smoke and engine exhausts. Food in the company
of wine becomes a joy to eat rather than a necessity of life.
The unexpected guest can always be given a royal welcome
when there is plenty of wine in the house, and there can
always be plenty of good wine in the house when you make
your own, for you make as much as you need, almost unaware
of the cost.

There is much, too, to be said for the making. There is as
much joy for the gardener in the growing of his own vegetables
as there is in the eating of his incomparably superior produce,
and so there is for the home winemaker. With knowledge and
forethought, making wine at home becomes an added pleasure. Little equipment is needed, the processes are simple,
the odd hour or so a week is sufficient for time and, with care,
the results are certain to please. This does not mean that you
simply take a short recipe, use the ingredients and methods
given and make a vintage wine. Neither can you take a packet
of seeds and a patch of earth and expect to grow superb
vegetables. For gardening you need to know something about

the soil and its needs, the kind of fertilizers required, the sort of cultivation preferred by the particular plant, watering, etc., etc., etc. In short, you need to know something about gardening as a whole if you are going to grow good quality plants that will give pleasure in the eating and nourishment in the digestion. So, too, with winemaking, you need to know something about the basic principles of preparation, fermentation and maturation, if you wish to get the greatest joys out of consumption.

These principles are all plain common sense based on a scientific knowledge of the activities that occur. For example, the recipes say 'add yeast'. But the yeast cell is a living organism that reproduces itself every three hours, provided all the circumstances are congenial, and during this reproduction the dissolved sugar is converted into ethyl alcohol and carbon dioxide gas. The yeast will also impart its flavour to the wine, so you begin to realize how important it is to provide the best circumstances for the yeast.

During the course of the ensuing chapters, it will be clearly and simply explained how to make good wine, and you are urged to read and learn these chapters thoroughly and to remember them as you work on the recipes provided at the end. It cannot be over-emphasized, however, that to make excellent wine it is far more important to understand the principles of preparation, fermentation and maturation, and to *apply* them to the recipe, than is the recipe itself. Two winemakers can make wine from the same ingredients and the same recipe, and the best wine will always be made by the one who knows most about making wine. This is, of course, equally true of commercial winemakers. You do not really need recipes, for you can always make a must from the ingredients that you happen to have available.

The quality will amaze you, as it does some of the most famous wine connoisseurs of the country. There is no doubt that the quality of the best wine made at home is as high as the quality of most of the best wine made commercially. Unhappily, not everyone who makes wine at home troubles to learn all that can be learned about winemaking. All too often they just knock up a gallon or so from a recipe that Mrs Cherry has given them, and everyone knows what lovely wine Mrs Cherry makes! But Mrs Cherry has learned all she can about making wine and blends skills and knowledge into her recipes.

As a result of too much concentration on recipes, some unnecessarily poor wine is still made at home and offered to guests who know better. But home winemaking is slowly obtaining the higher status symbol it so well deserves. More people than ever are joining winemaking clubs. More people are realizing the importance of properly understanding winemaking's simple methods, and troubling to buy, read and learn from such a book as this. You can be certain that if you do take the trouble to learn all you can about making wine at home, you will be delighted with the quality of your wine.

There is no difficulty about making wine at home. Only the simplest equipment is needed. The methods can be learned by a child, but they *must* be observed. The most common failing is impatience. So very many people expect immediate results and consequently offer wine that is still fermenting, has not yet cleared to brilliance, or has simply just not finished maturing. If you know something about the processes of making wine, you will realize that it cannot possibly be ready for drinking until all the essential changes have taken place. Consequently, you will leave it alone quietly to mature in the dark, and when the right time comes you will congratulate yourself on your wisdom. More about that in the proper place. Enough for now to show what is meant by learning about making wine and how much more important and valuable this knowledge is than a mere recipe.

2 It's all been done before

No one knows precisely who made wine first or when or where. The first recorded reference to making wine from grapejuice occurs about 2100 BC, and we know from the Old Testament that Sennacherib and Nebuchadnezzar planted extensive vineyards. Early Egyptian wall paintings show that wine was made then just as it is today, but it cannot have been so good, or the climate has changed, for no vines are grown in Egypt today. We know that the Pharaohs had wine with their meals and that the slaves and workers who built the Pyramids had a kind of beer made from grain. Both palm wine and date wine were also very popular at that time. There are extensive references to making wine in the Greek and later the Roman civilizations and we in fact get our word 'wine' from the old Greek word *oinos*. This was the produce of the fermented juice of the fruit of the *oine* – vine, to which pine cones, spices and herbs, and possibly honey as well, had probably been added to improve the flavour.

There is other evidence to believe that wine has in fact been made for maybe the past 10,000 years and that mead – a fermented solution of honey and water – has been drunk regularly for possibly as long as the past 12,000 years. Cider made by fermenting the juice of apples is also of ancient origin, for the word *seider*, akin to the Greek word *sikera*, is commonly used in the earliest records.

During the Greek and Roman civilizations, wine was one of the three chief items of trade – the other two being olive oil and grain. We know that the Greeks liked their drink somewhat spicy and in some of the country parts of Greece today the local wine is still so laced with spices and pine resin as to be almost undrinkable by those with more cultivated palates. The Romans preferred their wine diluted with water and disdained as uncouth those who drank their wine neat. The usual dilution was one part wine to three parts water. From the description that they left us of their orgies, the diluted wine must have been consumed in great quantities, for they frequently became drunk.

For at least 1,000 years before the birth of Christ, the Israelites had made wine by fermenting grapejuice. Their vats were carved out of the rocky ground at different levels, and runnels were made to allow for racking one to another – some of them can still be seen today. For centuries they had used wine as a symbol of the fruits of the earth with which to return thanks to God. The ritualistic eating of bread and drinking of wine on the eve of the Sabbath and other great feasts was a custom with which Our Lord grew up from childhood. It is possible, even probable, that as a young man He helped at times to make wine. He was also fully aware of its importance for social purposes, as is evidenced by His miracle at the Marriage Feast of Cana. His Church has consequently made enormous contributions to the improvements in techniques of wine growing and winemaking. The various religious orders planted vineyards wherever they went, improving the soil, organizing drainage or irrigation, training and pruning the vines, improving the stocks by hybridization, harvesting the grapes and making their wine. It seems only natural that the monks should also have experimented with distillation and flavouring with herbs to produce liqueurs that have become famous the world over.

In England, about AD 200, we know from an observer that, 'The rich drink wine from Italy or from around Marseilles. Poorer classes drink beer made from wheat and prepared with honey.' This revelation comes to us from the Deipnosophists of Athenaeus – an Egyptian collection of titbits of social gossip gathered together about the year AD 200.

Athenaeus also tells us about wines made in other areas. For example: 'Wine from Heraea (a town in Greece) drives men out of their senses and makes women inclined to pregnancy'; yet 'Wine from Cerauni (a town in Albania) causes sterility in women.'

Wine from Myndus (a port on the coast of the Aegean Sea) was prepared with sea water (2 per cent) and was an excellent aperient also aiding digestion of food.

Even today there are wines which are thought to have some special magic. There is, for example, a Hungarian wine called Somloi. It is a piquant and aromatic wine said by some to surpass even Tokay. Locally, the wine is thought to be conducive to the procreation of male children, and oddly enough there are more boys born in the district of Somló than there are girls, although in Hungary as a whole, there are more girl babies than boys! It is not obtainable in England at the time of writing ...

After the Romans left Britain we were invaded by the hard-drinking Angles and Saxons. Their two specialities were mead and ale. Being uncouth they used enormous cattle horns from which to drink their ale, and it is from this source that we get the tradition of drinking a yard of ale – a no mean feat! Mead was reserved for festive occasions and there is a delightful tale that during the four weeks after a wedding, the feastings were kept up with mead drinking and parties. It is suggested that this was the origin of our word 'honeymoon', but it may only be wishful thinking. At any rate, we do know that during the 1,000 years from about AD 200 to AD 1200, the main beverages were ale, mead and cider, and that some wine was imported from France, Spain and Portugal and possibly even from Italy too.

When Henry II married Eleanor of Aquitaine, however, the vast wine-producing area around Bordeaux became part of our realm, and the quantity of wine imported from that neighbourhood began to increase substantially. Subsequently this wine was to receive the general title of 'claret', derived from the French word *clairet*, meaning clear. Presumably much, if not all, of the other wine that was consumed was somewhat cloudy, hazy or to say the least, veiled.

Although many places in England today, especially in Gloucestershire and Norfolk, bear the name 'Vineyard' there would seem to be some evidence, at least, to suggest that these neighbourhoods grew cider apples rather than grape-bearing vines. The Greek word *sikera*, from which we get seider and now cider, meant any fermented liquor, not necessarily made from the grape. The Hebrew for sikera is 'shekar' which simply means 'strong drink'. When William the Conqueror imposed his new régime, many Olde Englishe words were supplemented by French words, sometimes with scant regard for accuracy. It could be as Worlidge suggested in 1676 that 'cider', the name of our principal fermented beverage, was changed to wine, which after all, at that time meant much the same thing – a fermented beverage or strong drink. Fermented grapejuice was rarely drunk in pure form, nearly always honey and spices were added and this is what the Greek word *sikera* often meant. It is known for certain that cider orchards were well developed and that excellent cider was produced. There seems to be no positive evidence either way, though the case seems most likely for cider-vineyards, for it is nowadays extremely difficult to grow good grapes that ripen fully out of doors in England.

In 1568 the first book on wine ever to be published in this country was written by one William Turner, a physician to Queen Elizabeth I. Wine was used extensively in the treatment of many ailments, both directly with medicinal and tonic values and also as a medium for drugs and herbs. One of the most common ailments of the day was the 'stone', and William Turner thought that this condition might be worsened by drinking red and heavy wines. He advocated, therefore, the drinking of white, and particularly Rhenish, wines. These wines from the Rhine were, as they are today, light and invigorating rather than intoxicating. Only a few copies of this precious book now exist, but a facsimile edition was printed in New York in 1941, and it is known that there are some copies, though hard to find, in England. The author would be glad to hear from any reader who has a copy that is no longer required.

It is interesting to note that all of the wines mentioned by Turner – and no others – are mentioned by Shakespeare in his plays. It would be not unreasonable to assume that Shakespeare used Turner's book for reference purposes.

The Middle Ages was a period of dynamic progress, and this involved increasingly greater social intercourse between people not yet accustomed to personal hygiene. Arnaldus de Villanova (1238–1314), one of the great doctors of his day, wrote a Rule of Health called *Regimen Sanitatis* dealing especially with food and wine and also bloodletting. This book was widely distributed throughout Europe, during the last quarter of the fifteenth century, by the earliest printers. The illustration on page 12 comes from a German edition of *Regimen Sanitatis* published in 1513. It shows a picture of 'the Queen of England' sitting naked in a bath of the period – presumably being bathed by her chambermaid – while a page or footman brings to her a 'porron' of wine. The purpose of the print was presumably to encourage people to wash their bodies regularly, and also to drink wine. The 'Queen of England' concerned may well have been Catherine of Aragon, but of this we cannot be sure. What we do know is that wine was even then regarded as a great benefit to healthy living.

Wines were often kept for a number of years, and resin was added to prevent souring but, in the main, new wine was preferred to old, which was usually sold somewhat cheaper at the then price of 3s a gallon. From the household records of the meals served at the Sovereign's expense to the Lords of the Privy Council meeting in the Star Chamber, it is clear that a substantial quantity of wine was drunk as well as a great deal of ale. There were, of course, many more staff assisting and waiting on the Lords than there were Lords themselves, and no doubt the staff had to be content with ale rather than wine. Sack (i.e. sherry), malmsey, muscatel and claret together with Rhenish wine were the best known and most frequently consumed.

All wine was, of course, free from any kind of tax, and when it was bought by the cask, ordinary table wine cost but 1d a pint. Mainly it was drunk in the evening after dinner, the last meal of the day; before that, ale would be used to wash down breakfast and lunch.

During the Michaelmas Law Term in 1590, when the

Lords of the Privy Council dined fifteen times in the Star Chamber, the bill for wines purchased for them was as follows:

55 gallons of the best Sack at 3s 4d a gallon
10 gallons of the best Muscadine at 3s 4d a gallon
20 gallons of the best old Rhennish at 3s 4d a gallon
10 gallons of the best new Rhennish at 4s 0d a gallon
10 gallons of the best Malmsey at 3s 4d a gallon

On 15 occasions, then, the Privy Councillors consumed 105 gallons of wine, equivalent to 42 bottles a day.

Little wine was made from English fruits and flowers, since imported wine was so cheap, and sugar was so dear and difficult to obtain. Mead was made from honey, which was commonly used only for sweetening, and fruit-flavoured meads are not as successful as those that are spiced. These spiced meads were very popular with the Celts who called the drink 'methaglyn', and it is still worth making today, though it needs to be sweet rather than dry. Mead and cider were very widely made in the country, and all the great houses had a stillroom in which mead, cider and ale were made and matured for the estate workers.

All the nobility had their favourite recipes and in 1669, Sir Kenelm Digbie made and published a collection of them. Sir Kenelm said that Hampshire honey was greatly esteemed, but that in his opinion, Norfolk honey was the best. He recommended one measure of honey to three of water, and boiled it steadily until one measure was boiled away. The gravity was checked by floating a fresh egg in the liquid when it was cool, and only the measure of a groat (a small coin of the period) must show. Next, herbs were added for flavouring, and these included violet leaves, strawberry leaves, sorrell, rosemary, balm, hart's tongue, liverwort, thyme and red sage. The whole was again brought to the boil and simmered for an hour, before spices, such as cloves, nutmegs and ginger were added. When the liquid was cool, yeast of beer or leaven of bread was added to start the fermentation. Sometimes 'Blue Raisins of the Sun' were added as well, and we can very well imagine the result to be a most potent drink. Sir Kenelm made cider by boiling a bushel of Pippin apples in 12 gallons of water, about 18 kg in 50 litres. When the liquid was cool it was strained and a pint of ale yeast was pitched into it. After two days of vigorous fermentation the young cider was racked, bottled and kept for two weeks before serving.

Towards the end of the seventeenth century, quite a number of books were published on the subject of winemaking and a few are well worth quoting. One of the best known is Walter Charleton's *Mysterie of Vintners*. He was a great advocate of racking to clear cloudy wines, and this practice is, in many opinions, still the best today. Charleton said, 'The best time to rack wine is the decrease of the moon and when the wine is free from fretting; the wind being at the North East or North West and not at South, the sky serene, free from thunder and lightening.' This advice was given again in another famous book in 1815, and was passed on to the author by an ancient winemaker as recently as 1945.

In 1676 a gentleman, J. Worlidge, wrote 'a treatise on cider and other wines extracted from fruits growing in this kingdom'. It was called *Vinetum Britannicum*, somewhat grandiose for the time, perhaps, but for anyone who has seen the Amateur Winemakers' National Show, such a title would well be justified today.

Worlidge was well educated, widely travelled, and able to express himself clearly, as the following quotation shows:

The cider made in Herefordshire, Gloucestershire and Worcestershire, being in great quantities carried to London and several other places of the Kingdom and sold at a very high rate, and valued above the wines of France, partly from its own excellency and partly from the deterioration of the French wines, which suffer in their exportation and from the sophistication and adulterations they receive from those that trade in them.

He was clearly a connoisseur of good wine and knew his way round, for there were also being published at that time numerous books giving advice on the 'sophistication and adulteration' of imported wines. It is abundantly evident that much of the wine being sold to the general public as claret or malmsey and so on, were in fact English wines, made from English fruits and flowers, blended with imported wines in the proportion of 3 measures of English to 1 of foreign. One can be shocked at the dishonesty of these merchants, but a little experimenting by yourself will show you that the result is an extremely good wine. This point will be expanded later under the heading of 'Blending', but in the meantime, do not be too hard on the merchants; after all, the customer thought it was worth buying!

Worlidge concedes that 'wine made from the grape is the richest drink this world affords', and he had evidently drunk it *in situ* before the 'deterioration of transportation', but he goes on to say that for our climate cider, perry, cherry and gooseberry wines, etc., etc., are better. This is a truth with which all those who have drunk deeply of good English wines as well as foreign wines will certainly agree.

Worlidge was in particular an authority on cider, and the methods he advocated are still used today. In his book he depicted presses, some of which may yet be still in use. He recommended scalding all containers in case 'they ferment the wine too violently and make it acid'. He used quicklime just as they do in Jerez today. Bacteria were called 'wild spirits' and he knew that they entered cracks in casks and existed in unscalded vessels. Brimstone was used for sterilizing, and he preferred the newly invented corks to glass stoppers, 'to enable the spirits to perspire' – a lovely phrase! He urged that fermented liquors be stored in sand while maturing, to enable an even temperature to be maintained. Worlidge was well accustomed to siphoning his wines and ciders when racking, and illustrates the siphon just as it is 300 years later. He also knew not only about the yeasts of both ale and bread, but also those which occurred naturally on the fruit. The former he regarded as 'too exciting', and preferred the latter.

Throughout his book, Worlidge frequently uses the word 'wine' to mean cider as though it were in fact an apple wine. This confusion, still current as late as 1676, gives further evidence to his theory that our ancient 'vineyards' were in fact cider orchards. Our 'wine yards' may well indeed have been planted with apple trees.

In recommending his excellent book, Worlidge condemned many English wines that he had tasted as being too sweet and lacking in alcohol, an admonition which is, alas, sometimes true today – 300 years on.

No mention is made of airlocks in these early books, though in 1691 another author by the name of Worth recommended the use of a pebble or stone on the bung-hole during fermentation so that the wine would not sour. Worth was an excellent winemaker, and one of his recipes is given in its proper place. Worth also describes the custom of fretting 'small wines' on rich lees and feeding the wine with 'sweet flesh'. 'Small wines' are thin, poor wines, lacking in body and flavour. 'Rich lees' is the deposit of strong full-bodied and well-flavoured wines. 'Sweet flesh' may be raisins, but there was also a custom that Charleton mentions in his book of feeding 'fretting wines', i.e. wines that are still fermenting, with raw beef. This was also a widely used custom by farmers making cider. It is well known, too, that in the days when those who kept inns also brewed their own beer, a cockerel would be 'flayed', i.e. killed, plucked and broken up into small pieces and added to a barrel of fermenting beer. When fermentation was finished, the beer was racked into another barrel, primed with a little extra sugar, allowed to mature for a few weeks and then served as a speciality of the inn. Hence the name 'Cock Inn'. A recipe is given later on and is strongly recommended as a superb drink.

The cause of fermentation was to be studied by many students in the years to come. It was thought by some that perhaps the wheat germ contained the 'spirit' of fermentation and in some old recipes a constant ingredient is three table-spoonfuls of flour – albeit wholemeal and stone-ground! In 1814 a somewhat pompous fellow called Cushing wrote *A Treatise on Family Wine Making* and said, 'Vinous fermentation may be said to be a Divine operation which the Omniscient Creator has placed in our cup of life, to transmute the fruits of the Earth into Wine for the benefit and comfort of His creatures.' Cushing had great faith if little knowledge, but his book, one of many similar, shows that family winemaking was a very well-established activity in 1814.

Apart from Worlidge there had as yet been no scientific study of making wine published in England, and so in 1816 John MacCulloch was invited to address the Caledonian Horticultural Society with a clear and closely reasoned study of winemaking as then known, though even MacCulloch admitted that very little was known about yeast. He knew that there was a fermenting substance in vegetable and fruit mucilage and in the germ cell of wheat. He knew that chemists had isolated a substance in these mucilages called 'azote', and that azotic gas was given off during fermentation. Another substance newly known to the research chemist was 'gluten', from which we get the word 'glutinous' – thick and sugary, sticky. Gluten had also been extracted from vegetable and fruit pulp as well as the wheat germ, and so MacCulloch guessed that azote and gluten were essential ingredients in fermentation.

Every ingredient used in the making of wine was studied with the same painstaking care. He condemned the excessive use of sugar and raisins and also the other common practice of the day, the addition of brandy. MacCulloch argues correctly that unless brandy is added during fermentation, it does not integrate with the wine, but only mixes with it. A French chemist had shown this by experiment only a year or so earlier. As a result of adding brandy after fermentation, the wine has a tendency to go flat and one can taste both the brandy and the flat wine separately. If you wish to fortify your wines, then, make a point of adding your spirit towards the end of fermentation, but not after. Fermentation will be slowed down and the wine will take longer to mature, as does port wine where the grape spirit is added during fermentation, but the result is far superior.

The great MacCulloch also recommended 'dry cold weather for racking as it is only then that wines are clear. They are generally turbid in damp, close weather and in southerly winds'.

Nearly twenty years later, in 1835, W. H. Roberts, a student of MacCulloch to whom he paid honour, wrote a splendid, practical book called *The British Winemaker*. In the first sentence he refers to *The Amateur Winemaker* and it is interesting to note that this phrase, lost for a century and a quarter, was regenerated in 1956. As many others before him, Roberts condemned oversweet wines and recommended the use of the saccharometer as an instrument for measuring the quantity of sugar in a liquid. At that time it cost 7s. Today known as the hydrometer, it costs around 70p, which is considerably cheaper, when you remember the difference in the value of money then and now. Roberts worked always from a specific gravity of 1·120, which with modern sugars would probably produce a medium-sweet and quite strong dessert wine. When Roberts was making wine he first checked the specific gravity of the fruit juice from which he was making his wine, then he added water amounting to twice the weight of the juice he had, and checked the specific gravity again. Then he added sufficient sugar to increase the specific gravity of his must to 1·120. He calculated that to increase the gravity by 35 he needed 1 lb sugar per gallon, i.e. 100 g per litre. It is probable that the sugar of 1835 was not quite as well refined as it is today, and contained a quantity of vegetable ash soluble in water. This would tend to give a higher reading than the actual sugar content justified, but even so Roberts's figures are pretty accurate and quite a good guide. He used his saccharometer every day and by this means could tell when fermentation started because the specific gravity began to drop. When the reading remained steady he knew that fermentation had stopped, so he racked and stoppered his wines, maturing them for several years.

Mr Roberts was a partner in a Scottish firm of brewers, and so had much professional knowledge available to him. It is greatly to his credit that he encouraged the amateur so generously.

In 1861 Mrs Beeton's first *Cookery and Household Management* book was published. It was mainly a collection of recipes of all kinds, and included many recipes (which we would now regard as poor) for making wine, but there is plenty of other evidence that good wine was made regularly in many parts of England. It was not so much a hobby as part of the normal domestic chores of the day, which included jam making, cake baking and so on. In early Victorian times it was a civilized custom to make and serve your wines as a speciality, and we know from her writings that Jane Austen was a dab hand at it.

It was the common practice to spread ale or bread yeast on toast and to float this on the must, covered up by several layers of butter muslin. The main disadvantage of this method was the danger of infection due to such a large surface of the wine being exposed to the air. A further disadvantage in this method is that the yeast usually multiplies rapidly without attenuating the must to any great extent. The result was usually a sweet wine of low alcohol content, to which brandy was added to remedy the deficiency. Hence nearly all the old recipes included brandy.

In the 1860s Pasteur discovered the yeast cell. Although further research was done in subsequent years by Professor Jaquemin in France and Professor Jørgenson in Denmark, the people who actually used yeast commercially were slow to use the pure cultures becoming available to them, and even to this day some amateur winemakers use granulated baker's yeast instead of the pure wine-yeast cultures so easily and readily available.

Although the habit of making wine at home almost died out between 1885 and 1945 during the three major wars, and the tremendous urban development that accompanied them, it has now returned. To the traditions of the past we can add improved methods based on scientific knowledge and make with confidence apéritifs, table wines, dessert wines and liqueurs that add graciousness to our modern living.

3 What you need: equipment

If you are gadget minded you will eventually find quite a few bits of winemaking equipment to do particular jobs particularly well. But they are by no means essential, although when you are already making good wine they may help you to improve the quality of your wine just a little more. Some few items, however, are very important, and although many of them are part of the normal kitchen equipment it is often a good practice to keep them separate for the purpose of making wine.

To start with you need a container in which to prepare your must, and a natural polythene bucket or bin will do the job admirably. These vessels can also be used for other purposes, of course, and even for the purpose for which they were designed, but it seems only common sense not to use for household refuse a container which you sometimes use for making wine. Let the point be taken without further ado.

Mashing vessels

First, then, you do need a vessel in which to prepare your must. A sound and thoroughly scrubbed wooden tub with a good lid was once used very widely, but these are heavy to move and hard work to scour, not to say quite expensive to buy. But they do last a lifetime, do not break or mark, and are kind to the must. Earthenware crocks that have been glazed inside are easy to clean though equally heavy to move about. It is best not to use old or foreign crocks in case they have been lead-glazed. This has a soft and honey-coloured look and sounds dull when tapped. The salt and other glazes look thin and hard and give off a sharper note when struck. These crocks come in a variety of sizes and shapes, but those which slope out and are extremely wide at the top are not as good as those which are almost upright and have a surface diameter of about 30 cm. These latter are the most easy to keep covered.

The natural polythene, combined mashing and fermentation bins are excellent. Sizes range from 5 litres to 50 litres (1 gallon to 11 gallons). They come complete with a carrying handle and a fitting lid. Some have removable grommets for the fitting of an airlock and a thermostatically controlled immersion heater. They are light to move, easy to clean, do not stain and do not affect the wine.

At this stage it should be emphasized never to use a metal container for any part of winemaking. The acids in the must and wine dissolve some of the metal and could produce a poisonous brew. Lead-glazed crocks used for making wine have been known to cause death to those who drank regularly of the wine made in them. Vessels made from iron, copper and zinc are also very dangerous and must not be used. Stainless steel, however, is quite safe. Highly coloured plastic bins should also be avoided since they may contain poisonous elements in the plasticizer. Cadmium has been used in yellow bins and may still be used where stringent controls are not enforced. Only natural polythene bins are completely suitable and then only for mashing and fermentation. Whilst inert to acids, it is thought that they could react with alcohol during prolonged storage. The danger from using unsuitable vessels is not so much that death may ensue, but rather that illness or sickness may be caused unnecessarily.

Masher

A long-handled wooden spoon is important and a masher is a useful extra. A masher consists of a cylinder of wood about 10 cm in diameter and about 25 cm long – in one end of which is inserted a broom handle. This obviously takes all the hard work out of breaking berries and fruits of all sorts and sizes. A jug with a graduated measure for liquids is also a useful possession, and here again plastic comes into its own.

Strainer

Next comes something in which to strain off the juice and press out the pulp. Any ordinary square of linen, tailor's canvas or the like will do, even a thoroughly cleaned flour bag; and one of these used in conjunction with a small press makes for greater efficiency. There are several small presses on the market, but a handyman can also devise a Heath Robinson type that works well.

Fermentation vessels

After straining and pressing you need something in which to ferment your must. The most widely used vessels are the 4·5 litre glass jars with a narrow neck to which two small handles are often fitted. You can see what's going on in them, they are easy to clean, they are cheap and easy to obtain but, being glass, need to be used with great care. Large glass or polythene carboys in a metal protecting-frame are very useful for those with plenty of space. Traditionally a cask was used and is still used commercially, but it seems likely that casks are now more often used at home for maturation – rather than fermentation.

Airlocks

Almost everyone nowadays uses an airlock, sometimes called a fermentation lock, of one kind or another. Their variety is almost legion. Many can be made up at home, others you can buy quite cheaply. They all work on the same principle of providing a barrier of water between the fermenting must and the outside air. A collection of differing types is illustrated.

Hydrometer

A really important piece of equipment which should be classed as essential is a hydrometer and trial jar. The use of this instrument will be discussed fully later on, but every wine-maker needs one to control the type of wine to be made.

Thermometer

As a further aid, a thermometer is very useful indeed, since you often need to know the temperature of your must or wine, but you can manage without it and still make good wine.

Vinometer

The vinometer is of such little use, even as a gadget, that it is hardly worth mentioning. It is supposed to measure the amount of alcohol in a finished wine, but whatever good it may be with a really dry wine, it is hopelessly inaccurate with a sweet wine, and the quantity of alcohol present in a wine can better be gauged from a careful record of your hydrometer readings.

Siphon

It is possible to pour wine from one container to another, but if the containers are large and heavy it is fairly difficult to do so without spilling some. You can buy a length of rubber tubing about 1 metre long to use as a siphon. Many winemakers have titivated this simple instrument with improvements of one kind and another, but basically there is no difference. Illustrations are shown.

Storage vessels

After racking, the fermented wine has to be stored for a period to mature. Most people, perhaps, use the same kind of jar as that in which they fermented their wine. Others prefer a stoneware jar which keeps out harmful light and maintains an even temperature. Best of all, however, is a cask. Any size from 28 to 50 litres is excellent, and they are not expensive for the advantages they give. Smaller casks are inadvisable, in that the ratio of the surface area of the wine in contact with air to the volume of wine is too great, and the wine spoils. Above 50 litres a full cask is a very heavy object and difficult to handle for a man or woman without special equipment and space. The cask is set on a little stand to ensure that the staves do not touch the ground or shelf, otherwise they would weep wine all over the place. A small wooden tap is an advantage, though the wine can be siphoned out if the cask is on a shelf.

Bottles

You will obviously need some bottles and corks. The bottles should preferably be normal wine bottles and not something previously used for orange squash or sauce. Corks for bottles and jars should ideally be new, but at least whole and sound, scrupulously clean and of good quality. Rubber bungs and plastic stoppers are now available. Although a little dearer to buy, they never wear out and can easily be sterilized. If you propose to bottle wine for long storage, cylindrical corks are needed, and a corker is essential. A simple type is illustrated.

Funnels

At all times a funnel will be found useful, indeed you can do with two or three of different sizes. A plastic one about 15 cm across at the top seems the best for most purposes, but a really large one can also be a great help.

Filters

The new type of white plastic filters now available are easy to use, quick and efficient. They are a vast improvement on the old canvas bags and the funnel filled with asbestos pulp. Most wines clear naturally but filters are useful for 'polishing' a veiled wine. Detailed instructions for their use are supplied with each kit.

Bottle brush

A good bottle brush about 40 cm long is almost essential. It will soon pay for itself by enabling you to use again previously used bottles and jars.

Record cards

A detailed record should be made of each wine, mentioning the date started, ingredients and quantities used, initial specific gravity and method followed. This information will prove of great value to you, enabling you to repeat the wines you enjoyed the most.

Labels and caps

Fancy labels are available to stick on your bottles, and to give a professional finish you can use plastic or metal-foil bottle caps.

Not really equipment because they are consumable, but if

you are going to make wine regularly, it is worth always keeping handy a bottle or two of Campden tablets or potassium
metabisulphite, some yeast nutrient tablets or ammonium
phosphate, some yeast in varieties and some citric acid crystals.
Some people also keep by them a small bottle of grape tannin.
You will also find many uses for a packet of unmedicated
cotton wool.

This list of equipment is by no means exhaustive, nor is it
by any means *all* essential. You must have a mashing vessel, a
fermentation jar, an airlock, a storage jar, a hydrometer, a
piece of rubber tube, some wine bottles and corks and a
funnel. The rest you can add as you please.

All the wine-equipment firms, whose names and addresses
are listed as an appendix, issue catalogues and price lists. They
will be delighted to send you a copy.

4 What you need: ingredients

Important minors

Flavour Wine can be made from almost any non-poisonous plant, but after a period of experiment the tendency seems more and more to concentrate on fruit wines. Flowers used with discretion can give delicate bouquet and flavour to a wine, but lack acid, tannin and nitrogenous mucilage, which need to be added. Vegetables and cereals have plenty of mucilage and starch, but lack acid and tannin. Herbs, leaves, etc., give only flavouring and perhaps some tannin, and we are back to fruit again for the rest.

The grape has everything: flavour, mucilage, acid, tannin, nutrient and even yeast all built in, as it were. With other fruit there is generally some imbalance, and it is often necessary to correct the deficiency by addition or dilution. The most frequent correction is to the acid. Most of our fresh fruit has an acid content too high for the juice alone to be used, and it has to be diluted. That is one reason why water is always added in our recipes. The other reason is to leach out the flavour from the pulp. To assist this process of flavour extraction from fruit, it has been found beneficial to add a pectin-destroying enzyme to all fruit musts at the outset of the mashing stage, but this will be dealt with more fully later on.

Acid There is always a variety of different acids such as citric, tartaric and malic in fruit, but after dilution it is often necessary to add some more. If there is a shortage of acid as in flower, vegetable and cereal wines, either citric or tartaric acid must be used. Malic acid can also be used with good effect, and you can now buy packets of these three acids mixed in a suitable ratio. Citric acid is frequently used in the form of lemon juice, and some recipes include lemons.

When a recipe calls for the rind and juice of one or more lemons or oranges, it is important to omit the white pith, which imparts a bitter taste to the wine. The thin skin can be peeled very easily with a fruit or potato peeler, and the orange or lemon is then cut across the middle and the juice is squeezed in the usual way, but keep out the pips.

Tartaric acid is usually added in the form of tartaric acid crystals. The advantage of using tartaric acid is that although soluble in water, tartaric acid precipitates in alcohol to form cream of tartar crystals, these cling to the bottom and side of the fermentation jar and are left behind when the wine is racked. Malic acid is frequently converted, by a malo-lactic ferment caused by bacterium gracile, into lactic acid which has a less acid taste than malic acid. Thus the yeast is provided with an adequate acid background without making the finished wine taste too sharp.

With less than 2 parts acid per thousand, wine tastes 'medicinal' and will not keep. With more than 10 parts acid per thousand, wine tastes excessively tart and takes a long time to mature. The optimum seems to be from four to seven parts per thousand, depending on the type and purpose of the finished wine. A dry wine would need to have not more than five parts of acid per thousand, while a sweet wine would need seven parts per thousand. When it is known that a must has no acid at all as in flower and vegetable, cereal and some dried fruits like dates, then it is easy to calculate the right amount of acid to add. The addition of 25 g tartaric acid to 5 litres of must increases the acid content by 0·5 per cent.

When it is known that there is some acid present, the problem is a little more difficult. The recipes given at the end of this book have taken this matter into account for you, but if you are sufficiently interested you can buy a simple acidimetric outfit or, though much less accurate, you can use a BDH Narrow Range pH indicator paper, which gives some guide and covers an adequate working range. With the acidimetric outfit you will receive full instructions and you need to aim at an acid content of your must of about 0·5 per cent. With the pH paper, you need to obtain a colour reaction equivalent to between pH 3 and 4. A little trial and error with a sensitive tongue achieves a rough guide, but acid is the 'cornerstone' of bouquet and flavour. It is worth taking a little trouble to get it right.

During maturation, the different acids in the wine combine with the alcohol to form first aldehydes and then acetaldehydes and so on, in an even more complex chain of esters. Each year of maturation some of the acid is used up, and so clearly a wine that starts off low in acid will not keep well. While, on the other hand, a wine that is high in acid will take longer to mature.

Tannin Most fruits have tannin in their stalks and skins, some much more than others. Tannin gives character and a subtle bitterness to a wine, adding stability and life. A wine will not keep many years without plenty of tannin. At present there is no easy means of checking tannin content apart from taste, but if you suspect that a wine is going to be 'flabby', and lacks tannin, then you can add $\frac{1}{2}$ tsp prepared grape tannin for every 6 bottles of wine being made.

Nutrient Just as soil needs fertilizer, so too does yeast. Some winemakers are content with acid and the nitrogenous matters in the fruit pulp, others add a prepared nutrient tablet or a small teaspoonful of ammonium phosphate per gallon. There are a number of yeast energizers and branded nutrients available and all are good, especially Tronozymol, which also includes added vitamins and mineral salts. There is no doubt that if you use a nutrient you do get a better fermentation and one that more surely converts all the sugar to alcohol and carbon dioxide.

You will see that all the recipes given in this book recommend the addition of 'nutrient'. The actual type you use is a matter for your own choice and preference, perhaps depending in the long run on your purse.

Water There is constant controversy about the advantage of using cold, boiled water as against boiling water. It is not a good thing to use cold water straight from the tap in case it contains any wild yeast or bacteria that will develop upon standing. Cold water is said to retain the natural flavours better than hot water which might dissipate them. On the other hand, hot water helps to leach out the flavours and goodness more efficiently than cold. Most winemakers do, in fact, use boiling water, and it does not appear to matter much whether the water is 'hard' or 'soft' – though this factor is important when making beer. Bitter beer needs added salts as found in hard water, while stouts and brown ales are better when made with soft water.

Essential majors

Sugar Like so many other things, sugar was discovered by the Romans, although it was not imported into England until 1264 by Henry III at a cost of £10 per lb. Small quantities were refined here after the middle of the sixteenth century, but it did not become cheap and plentiful for another 200 years. Chemically, there are many forms of sugar: sucrose, glucose, fructose, maltose, etc., etc. You will perhaps only know of lump sugar, soft sugar, demerara sugar, preserving sugar, caster sugar, sugar pieces and so on. These are, in fact, all sucrose in different dress! Any of them do for winemaking, though soft sugar is cheapest and the easiest to handle, and therefore most often used. Demerara can be used for dark wines, but the caramel in it imparts colour and some flavour to the wine, so it is inadvisable to use it with light and delicate wines. It is essential to use brown sugar or some caramel when making a Madeira type wine, to obtain the characteristic flavour.

Soft sugar – sucrose – is a combination of glucose and fructose. An enzyme present in yeast, called invertase, causes the two sugars to split apart.

In brewing beer commercially, a sugar called invert sugar is always used, and some amateur winemakers prefer to use invert sugar in their wine musts. Invert sugar is sucrose inverted, or split up, into a simple mixture of glucose and fructose. Yeast is unable to ferment sucrose direct, but can readily use glucose and fructose. It is argued that fermentation begins sooner and is more successful if this splitting up is done for the yeast. In fact, the sugar splits by itself in the presence of the enzyme invertase, which is always present in yeast. However, those who would like to invert their sugar artifically can do so simply by bringing to the boil 1 kg of sugar with 1 level teaspoonful of citric or tartaric acid in 60 cl of water and simmering this syrup for 20 minutes. This makes 1 litre.

It is important to make sure that all the sugar used is thoroughly dissolved in a must, and some winemakers always add it in syrup form for convenience, since the dry crystals cause foaming. If these are used, remove some of the wine, dissolve the sugar in it, and pour it back slowly into the jar.

Yeast Leaven of bread and ale yeast had been known for thousands of years, but it wasn't until 1837 that Cagniard Latour in France, and Schwann in Germany demonstrated that beer and wine yeasts were spherical bodies able to multiply, and that the cells belonged to the vegetable world needing nitrogenous matter as well as sugar to enable them to live and grow. Schwann called these cells *Zuckerpilz*, which means sugar fungi. In the same year another worker, von Meyen, suggested the name *Saccharomyces* as a generic name for Schwann's sugar fungi.

The chemists of the day, however, had different views on the causes of fermentation. Some thought it was caused by oxygen, others that spontaneous generation was responsible. The controversy was not settled until Pasteur conducted his epic research work on sterilization. He proved that when a yeast which had been grown in a pure and germ-free medium was introduced into a pasteurized beer wort, it caused fermentation, thus proving beyond doubt that yeast alone was the cause.

His work was taken up by others, especially in France and Denmark. Later, it was discovered that an enzyme called zymase was actually the catalyst which enabled the sugars to split into alcohol and carbon dioxide, and that zymase is produced by the yeast and secreted through the cell wall. The presence of healthy yeast cells is therefore imperative to fermentation. The science of fermentology was actually founded then, over 100 years ago, but research work still continues on this subject. Recently, for example, it has been shown that yeasts which have been submitted to a small dose of radiation give a better fermentation and flavour than those not so treated. Radio-multivure yeasts as provided by Fermenta are not themselves radioactive and can be used with perfect safety.

Yeast needs oxygen to enable it to grow and reproduce itself, and it can get this most easily from the air. There is usually enough oxygen mixed in with the must for the yeast to use this at first and so to multiply rapidly, but in this aerobic state, as it is called, very little alcohol is produced. It is for this reason that in winemaking we cut off the oxygen supply from the atmosphere by means of an airlock. When there is no free oxygen available the yeast is able, through the enzyme complex called zymase which it produces, to break down the sugar molecules so as to obtain a further supply of oxygen. The yeast is now living in its anaerobic state (i.e. without air) and in doing so forms from any given quantity of sugar about 47 per cent alcohol and 48 per cent carbon dioxide. The remaining 5 per cent it uses itself. The alcohol stays in solution in the wine, the carbon dioxide, being a gas, floats to the surface in little bubbles which burst on the surface, causing a slight hissing noise. These are just two of the signs of fermentation, the visible bubble and the audible hiss.

Yeast cells are elliptical, spherical or pointed: at least the yeasts with which we are particularly concerned are so shaped. There are many hundreds of different yeasts and happily we are concerned only with three of them. Our three have special

names, although all three of them begin with the generic title
Saccharomyces. They are:

Saccharomyces apiculati or wild yeast.
Saccharomyces cerevisiae or ale and bread yeast.
Saccharomyces ellipsoideus or wine yeast.

All these yeasts have many different varieties, and the variety
commonly used for bread is different from that used in brewing although they are of the same type.

The difference between *S. cerevisiae* (bread and ale yeast)
and *S. ellipsoideus* (wine yeast) is considerable. When making
bread and beer it is important to obtain a very rapid fermentation. In breadmaking the dough is left for only $1\frac{1}{2}$ to 2 hours
to rise, and in this time sufficient carbon dioxide has to be
released to form the honeycomb of a slice of bread. In beer-
making the enormous vats are left uncovered so that the yeast
can ferment from the top of the beer, obtaining much of its
oxygen in an aerobic state and thus reproducing itself very
rapidly. A speedy fermentation is obviously necessary to prevent the growth of other yeasts, fungi and germs, and because,
like bread, large quantities of beer are consumed, it must of
necessity be made quickly.

With *S. ellipsoideus* (wine yeast) we achieve a different purpose. This yeast ferments slowly from the bottom of a sugar
solution and in an anaerobic state. This increases the quantity
of alcohol produced. Because of the slower fermentation delicate esters and flavours are retained rather than dissipated,
and the result is altogether finer than beer which is funda-
mentally a long, thirst-quenching drink rather than a nectar
to be admired and savoured.

The variety of wine yeast indigenous to southern Spain,

where sherry is made, is different from the varieties found in Bordeaux, Champagne, Burgundy, Germany, Italy, etc. In each area the different variety yields a subtlety of flavour which is quite distinguishable.

As has already been stated, yeast cells belong to botany rather than biology. They are invisible to the naked eye, but can clearly be seen under the microscope. They look rather transparent, with one or two opaque dots in them and a bud on the side. Their actual size is about $\frac{7}{1000}$ millimetre and when they grow to about $\frac{10}{1000}$ millimetre the bud separates and starts its own life. A bud takes about three hours to grow large enough to break off and will reproduce itself some thirty times before dying of old age! In 36 hours, then, one cell will have become 4096 cells and still have another 2 days to live! Since the minimum count of viable cells in a sachet of yeast is in excess of 1 million, it can be seen that within 36 hours there are more yeast cells in a jar of fermenting wine than there are human beings on earth.

When the cell dies it decomposes and one of the substances released is nitrogen which the living yeasts use. This process is called autolysis. The remaining decomposition has to be removed at the end of fermentation by racking the wine from the lees. If the wine were not so racked an unpleasant taste would develop in the wine caused by these dead yeast cells which had decomposed.

It should be noted that the actual yeast cell itself does not ferment the sugar. What happens is that when a molecule of sugar, $C_6H_{12}O_6$, comes into contact with the complex of enzymes known as zymase, the molecule of sugar splits into 2 molecules of ethyl alcohol and 2 molecules carbon dioxide as shown by the following chemical characters, $C_6H_{12}O_6 \rightarrow 2CO_2 + 2C_2H_5OH$. The zymase is not used or changed or combined. Its very presence causes the break up of the sugar molecule and so it is said to act as a catalyst.

The most striking observation about enzymes is their specific character. Each one serves a different purpose and catalyses a different reaction. No one enzyme can cause more than one action.

Thus the presence of the enzyme known as maltase, causes maltose to break down into sucrose. The presence of the enzyme known as invertase causes sucrose to split into fructose and glucose and, as you already know, the presence of zymase causes these sugar molecules to split up into alcohol and carbon dioxide at the end of a long and complicated process.

The wonderful yeast cell produces all these enzymes in itself and many other substances, not yet fully understood, that develop individual flavours in wines. Many of these occur during the process of autolysis, or self digestion. When a yeast cell dies the regular normal transformations which are necessary for the maintenance of life will cease; but the activity of the enzyme does not cease with the death of the cell and therefore chemical transformations resulting from the un-restricted action of the enzymes occur in the dead cell, and the resulting products include a long series of amino acids, the fundamentals of life itself.

5 How to do it: theory

The making of wine can be fairly easily divided into three stages: Preparation, Fermentation and Maturation.

Preparation includes all the activities up to the addition of the yeast.

When the yeast is added fermentation begins and is the process which then continues up to the first racking.

When the wine is racked and put into store – maturation begins and includes all other activities up to the day the wine is declared ready for drinking.

Preparation

The methods of preparation vary with the kind of wine being made. In most wines it is sufficient to wash the fruit clean from dirt and dust, to break it up into small pieces and to pour boiling water on it. This mash is then left to soak for a couple of days so that the colour, flavour and goodness can be extracted from the fruit. If any of the fruit is overripe, and in any case as a precaution against infection, it is a good rule always to add 1 Campden tablet per 5 litres. This little tablet in solution gives off sulphur dioxide which effectively sterilizes the must by killing off unwanted bacteria and wild yeasts. Happily, it has no harmful effect on the cultured yeast which we use.

A spoonful of pectic enzyme will assist the process of extraction and help to produce a brilliantly clear wine. What happens is this: the fruit juice is contained in cellular walls and not all of these are ruptured when the fruit is crushed. Yet some are broken so small that they are carried into the wine, making it cloudy. On the skin of most fruits there is an enzyme called pectinase which effectively destroys this cellular matter. This enzyme is itself destroyed by heat and yet hot water as opposed to cold aids in the sterilization of the fruit and especially in the extraction of the flavour, etc. For this reason it is as well to add the Campden tablet and the pectic enzyme as soon as the must is cool, so that the artificial pectinase can reinforce the natural enzyme in destroying the pectin, and the sulphur dioxide can keep the must sterile.

Some winemakers rely exclusively on cold water and pectic enzyme, arguing that their wine has a better flavour, but this method has not yet found unanimous approval. At the other extreme there are those who boil their fruits to extract the greatest goodness. This policy also cannot always be recommended. The result is sometimes a wine that will not clear, and even one with an overpowering and possibly unacceptable flavour. A better answer is fermentation on the pulp. Boiling water is poured on to the fruit which is mashed and left to cool. Then pectic enzyme and Campden tablets are added, the bin is covered and left for 24 hours while the enzyme breaks up the pectin. Next day an active yeast is added and when fermentation starts is continued for 4 days or so. Each day the pulp must be pressed down to keep it moist and keep it free from infection. After 4 days the pulp is strained, pressed and discarded, more sugar is added and the fermentation is continued in a jar fitted with an airlock.

It will be realized that different fruit has to be treated differently to some extent. For example, you can crush grapes or currants or cherries or plums with your fingers, but apples are too hard. Fruit of this kind can be cut into sections, or better still broken with a masher described in the chapter on equipment. Such fruit should be dropped at once into water containing some citric acid crystals and a crushed Campden tablet to prevent browning – oxidation – which taints the wine unpleasantly. Many dried fruits are easily broken up with a mincer and it is a help to treat grain in the same way. Hard stone fruits or gooseberries soften after a few hours steeped in hot water, and it will be found that they can be crushed with the hands when the liquid is cool. This is another good reason, of course, for pouring on boiling water.

In an earlier chapter reference was made to lids for mashing vessels and this point is of paramount importance. It is absolutely essential to keep a close-fitting clean cover over wine in all its stages, from the moment you start the preparation until the moment it goes into your glass. During mashing keep your vessel well covered with something substantial. Butter muslin is not enough. A sheet of polythene held down with a rubber ring or tied down with thin string keeps out not only dust and dirt but, even more important, bacteria and fungi spores, particularly the vinegar germ – *Mycoderma aceti* – which can ruin your must irretrievably.

Having extracted the juice and flavour from your basic ingredients the must now has to be adjusted for acidity, tannin and sugar. Mention has already been made about acidity and tannin on pages 41 to 43 and it is sufficient here to remind you not to forget them. The nutrient (see page 43) can also go in now, but before you add the sugar it is important to use your hydrometer.

The hydrometer was first used as far back as about 1786, and although its use was recommended by Roberts in 1835 and by many more recent writers, there are still far too many amateur winemakers who do not possess or use one – and yet it is probably the most useful piece of equipment there is in winemaking. Without it we have no control over the sugar content of our must and are more than likely to make a cloyingly sweet cordial rather than a good strong wine. The sugar content of different fruits varies enormously – not only from each other but also from year to year. As a result a recipe that is appropriate one year, may well contain too much or too little sugar another. Only the hydrometer can tell us just what these differences are, so that we are enabled to adjust the quantity of added sugar as necessary.

In its modern form, the hydrometer is a glass cylinder consisting of a long, narrow neck and a slightly thicker and shorter base. The base is weighted and from 5 to 8 cm long and about 2 cm in diameter. The neck is from 12 to 18 cm long and about 1 cm in diameter. It contains a graduated scale and is illustrated in the photographs.

The purpose of the hydrometer in winemaking is to determine the amount of sugar in a given volume of a must or wine and from this we can calculate the potential amount of alcohol the wine would contain if fermentation were continued to the limit. The weight of a cubic foot of water at 15°C is approximately 1,000 oz and so the top of the graduated scale in the hydrometer is marked 1·000. When a hydrometer floats in water at 15°C the level of the water cuts this 1·000 line.

When sugar is added to water, the solution becomes thicker and heavier and this causes the hydrometer to float higher with more of its neck sticking out of the liquid. The line at which it floats shows the weight of the sugar solution relative to an equal volume of water, whose weight we know. By subtracting the weight of the water we are thus able to find the weight of the sugar. To save these calculations, each hydrometer is accompanied by a set of tables showing in parallel columns (a) the specific gravity reading, (b) the equivalent weight of the sugar in solution and (c) the potential quantity of alcohol that will be produced if all the sugar is used up during the fermentation. These tables can never be exactly accurate, because at the top end there may be some slight obscuration because of the other suspended solids, and at the lower end because of the dilution of the water by the alcohol which is less heavy than the water.

However, the tables at the back of the book are as nearly accurate as it is possible to make them.

If the temperature of the must or wine is much varied from 15°C then some corrections must be made to the reading as indicated with the tables.

To use the hydrometer take it from its box and make sure that it is thoroughly clean, and the trial jar also. Then place the instrument in the jar, being careful not to let it drop to the bottom; both are glass and can be easily broken with careless handling. Next take some of your must and pour it into the jar until the hydrometer just floats. If it sinks low there is very little sugar present, if it floats high you have a good deal of natural fruit sugar in your must. The actual reading taken at eye level can be compared with the tables given to tell you exactly how much sugar you have and therefore, by subtraction from your intentions, how much more sugar to add. For example: Suppose you are making apple wine and that your must has a reading of 1·035 – this indicates that you have already in your wine 397 grammes of natural sugar by weight per gallon of must – 4·54 litres. Suppose also that you wish to make a table wine of the sauterne type; you need about 12 per cent alcohol and some residual sugar for sweetening. First of all you will see by further reference to the tables given that to achieve an alcohol content of 12 per cent you need a starting specific gravity of 1·088, which is equal to 970 grammes of sugar in a gallon (4·54 litres) of must. Since we already have almost 400 grammes sugar in our supposed must we in fact need only a further 370 grammes for a fermentation to 12 per cent alcohol. When the wine has fermented out, another 100–200 grammes sugar per 4·54 litres can be dissolved with a little of the finished wine and then returned to the jar after racking. It is always possible, if there is still plenty of acid and nutrient left, for the wine to start fermenting again, but by racking the wine from its lees beforehand, adding 2 Campden tablets per 4·54 litres and removing the jar to a cool place, it is unlikely that further action will occur, and two or three frequent rackings will stabilize the wine.

No recipe can give you such exact figures, because the natural sugar content of your must can vary tremendously, both with the kind of fruit you are using and with your success in extraction during the mashing. This is the very reason why a hydrometer is so important. With it you can control precisely the wine you are making, sweet or dry, strong or not so strong, table or dessert. Without it you take literally 'pot luck'. Furthermore, with a hydrometer you can if needs be check the progress of your wine, and when fermentation stops you can tell in an instant whether you have a stuck ferment or whether the wine is finished. If at the end of fermentation you take another hydrometer reading and find that the specific gravity of your wine is 1·000 or less, you may be sure that you have had a successful ferment.

While it is necessary to follow through the discussion on the hydrometer you will remember that it arose from the quantity of sugar to add to a must to produce the type of wine you required. Having decided the exact amount of sugar to add, you dissolve it in the must by stirring thoroughly. It is important not to leave sugar particles in the bottom of the jar because otherwise they may remain there and never get into solution. If you are using a sugar syrup it is important not to use quite so much water in the mashing.

Now comes the addition of the yeast and the fixing of the airlock. Sometimes, especially if there is much fruit sludge in the must, the early stages of fermentation are tumultuous. Accordingly, then, it is as well not to fill the jar too full, and so leave a little room for expansion. Allowing enough space for, say, ·25 litre of liquid is usually enough. Surplus must can be put into a bottle beside the jar and the latter topped up in due course.

Before inserting an airlock in the cork and the cork in the neck of the jar, you must add the yeast. This can be done in a variety of ways for wine yeast comes in many forms. It can be bought in foil-encased capsules of pressed dried yeast; in a foil sachet of dried yeast granules – with or without nutrient salts – sufficient for one fermentation of from 5 to 25 litres; in a 100 gramme bottle of loose dried granules – with or without nutrient salts –; in a transparent polythene sachet containing yeast cells in distilled water – again sufficient for one fermentation; or as a yeast culture on an agar jelly slant in a sealed test tube. These yeasts are all true wine yeasts of named subvarieties for the different wine types, e.g. hock, burgundy, champagne, sauternes, sherry. Each packet, or bottle or tube, is accompanied by directions for use. Generally the idea is to re-activate the yeast in ·25 litre of fruit juice before adding it to the must.

The bottle to be used for this purpose must be carefully sterilized beforehand. A solution of fruit juice – any kind will do – is boiled with a spoonful of sugar and a small portion of nutrient. This is then poured into the prepared bottle which should never be more than half full, plugged with cotton wool and allowed to cool. When the temperature is down to 24°C the yeast is added and the whole shaken up. The cotton wool plug is replaced and the bottle is left in a warm place for a day or two. Soon a splendid surge of bubbles will be seen rising to the surface and this means the yeast is alive and well. It may now be added with confidence to the must and fermentation will start almost immediately. A little water should, of course, be placed in the trap of the airlock and as fermentation continues large lozenges of colourless carbon dioxide gas will be seen escaping.

Since it takes a little while to reactivate a yeast, it is as well either to keep a starter bottle always ready or else to prepare the starter a day or two before you need it. The starter bottle can be kept going for many months simply by using only two-thirds of the quantity of liquid at ony one time, and making up the total again with some more fruit juice, acid and nutrient, boiled and cooled in sterile conditions of course. The starter bottle should be gently shaken from time to time and again immediately before adding to a must, so as to stir up the yeast. Some of the new granulated yeasts and nutrients, such as the Unican Super Yeast and the CWE Formulae 67 are extremely effective and can be re-activated in a matter of hours in the right conditions.

As was mentioned earlier the yeasts can be obtained in a variety of wine types and there is general agreement that some yeasts, particularly champagne and sherry, when used in conjunction with a suitable must, do give a pronounced flavour of the wine to which that yeast is indigenous. Other flavours are more subtle, but the cultivated palate can certainly tell the difference, especially when the type of wine is imitated with

a carefully selected and sympathetic must. A basic ingredient
with a pronounced bouquet – such as elderflower or raspberry
– is unlikely to take on any yeast flavour. Furthermore, it
would be hopeless to try to graft the flavour of a Johannis-
berger yeast, for example, on to a blackberry or elderberry.
Common sense must be used in this matter and guidance has
been given with the recipes.

Fermentation

Preparation is now complete and the must will ferment into
wine without any interference provided it is kept in a warm
but not too hot place. From 20–24°C seems the ideal. It is
sufficient to keep an eye on the jar from time to time and
to make a detailed record of the wine for future reference.

This record is well worth making and keeping, especially
in the beginning. You need to note the names and quantities
of all your ingredients including sugar, water, acids, nutrients
and yeast; the method of preparation, the day you started, the
first specific gravity reading, and the adjusted specific gravity
after an addition of sugar. This gives you a good idea of the
amount of natural sugar present in different fruits and enables
you to compare them, one year with another. When fermentation is finished note the final specific gravity and record the
date of first racking and second racking, and so on, and finally,
a note describing the finished wine. Many winemakers use a
luggage label, which they tie on to the neck of their fermentation jars, but you can also buy a printed card reminding you
of the details to keep.

Mention has already been made of the process of fermenting on the pulp. It was customary to reserve this method for
dark-red wines but many winemakers now always use it when
making fruit wines.

When the fruit is mashed and the boiling water poured on, the bin is covered while the must cools. As soon as the temperature is down to 24°C or so, additional acid, nutrient, tannin and the activated yeast are added. The whole mash ferments for 4 or 5 days, no more. The pulp is lifted up to the top of the jar by the rising carbon dioxide and so must be pressed down two or three times daily to keep the pulp ('cap' as it is called in this instance) in the must, so that the goodness can be extracted, and to prevent the vinegar bacteria getting a hold. The must is then strained into a clean fermentation jar and the pulp is squeezed dry, the sugar is added and stirred until dissolved. An airlock is fitted and fermentation is continued in the usual way.

This method ensures a thorough extraction of colour and goodness and there is little risk from exposing the surface of the must to the air if it is carefully and closely covered. It is the standard commercial practice in the preparation of red wine from black grapes and can be equally recommended in the making of fruit wine at home.

There are some differences of opinion about the merits of what is known as a high temperature ferment and a low temperature ferment. Obviously, in some hot countries like the South of Spain, North Africa and California, fermentation is carried on with the surrounding temperature at nearly 28°C, even in October. The ferment is tumultuous and quickly finished so that within eight or ten days the new wine can be racked into casks to begin the process of maturation. The especial advantage of this commercially is that the must is less likely to become infected, mainly because it is not standing about for so long as with a slower ferment. On the other hand, with a slower, more gentle ferment, delicate esters and flavours are less likely to be lost, and provided the must is adequately protected from bacterial infection, there is reason to believe that a slower ferment at a somewhat lower temperature produces the better wine. At home this point is rather academic except when fermenting on the pulp, since the process of fermentation is carried on under an airlock which completely protects the wine. If you can ferment your wine at home in a fairly steady 20°C you will be providing the best temperature for your yeast.

Another aspect of fermentation worthy of special attention is the technique of adding sugar at intervals. Yeast becomes oppressed if the specific gravity of the must is too high, and fermentation is sometimes difficult to start. The question doesn't arise with table wines, since it is important that they do not contain too much alcohol – 10–12 per cent is ample. Accordingly, then, an original specific gravity of between 1·075 and 1·088, which is ideal for the yeast to start, is also sufficient for the finished wine. But for dessert wines, which need to be stronger and sweeter, it is better to add additional sugar during fermentation than to put it all in at the beginning. Start your wine as you would for a table wine, but arrange to take hydrometer readings after eight days and then every two days. When the specific gravity falls to 1·004–1·006 take out some wine and dissolve in it some additional sugar. As a rule of thumb, 56 grammes of sugar will raise the gravity in 4·5 litres by about 5. Experience teaches that only 112 grammes should be added to 4·5 litres a time. It should never be added dry, since this causes foaming and loss. Subsequently, the sugar crystals remain undissolved at the bottom of the jar. Even in solution, the sugar should be added carefully. You should remember, too, that the sugar is going to occupy some bulk space and a little extra wine should be withdrawn from the jar to allow for this.

When making wine you will find that nearly all recipes make up into nearly 5 litres – most gallon jars hold between 4.8 and 5 litres anyway. The extra must is fermented in a bottle beside the jar – a good plug of cotton wool serves as an airlock. When the time for racking comes, this extra wine will be found most useful for topping up the new jar. During fermentation the bottle can also take the little drops of wine displaced by the added sugar.

By careful watch of frequent hydrometer readings sometimes three or four extra doses of sugar can be added to a fermenting wine. As fermentation slows down, the last addition can be of a smaller quantity of sugar. If your intention is to make as strong a wine as possible, continue fermentation to the point where the yeast is completely inhibited by the quantity of alcohol formed. At the same time the amount of residual sugar should not exceed a hydrometer reading of say 1.015–1.020, depending on how sweet you like a sweet wine. Remember that alcohol is thinner than water and therefore that a strong wine with a specific gravity of 1.000 will in fact contain some sugar.

In the normal way yeast cells will go on living happily, secreting zymase to split the molecules of sugar into alcohol and carbon dioxide gas, reproducing themselves and dying. If fermentation stops, one of several different events have happened. These are as follows:

1 Liquid gets too hot The very activity of fermentation itself generates some heat, about 4°C, so if the temperature around the jar is 26°C the temperature of the wine is about 30°C. At this level the yeast often finds life hard and slows down considerably. If the temperature goes up to 50°C, the yeast is killed.

2 The liquid gets too cold In the same way that life gets hard for the yeast when the temperature rises too high, so too does it get tough when it falls too low. A new strain of lager yeast, said to be able to ferment at about 5°C is now on the market, but the vast majority of yeasts just go on strike at this temperature. Experiment has shown that they like the continual temperature to be about 20–24°C, and clearly this is a matter over which we have some control. Fermenting jars should be kept in an evenly warm place.

3 All the sugar has been used up This usually only occurs when a fermentation is finished. If you have used a hydrometer and know exactly how much sugar has been used, you can try adding a little more. It may start the fermentation again; at worst it will slightly sweeten an otherwise dry wine.

4 All the nutrient has been used up If you have taken the precaution of adding nutrient to the must at the same time as the sugar and yeast, this problem is not likely to arise. Tronozymol, or a similar yeast energizer, usually takes care of this problem and will often restart a wine that has stopped fermenting for this reason.

5 All the acid has been used up Some ingredients such as flowers, cereals, vegetables and dried fruits are so lacking in acid that if you have not added sufficient at the beginning, then the yeast will give up. Yeast, like some other plants, insists on a slightly acid solution in which to grow. Fermentologists say that the optimum degree of acidity for fermentation of wine is between pH 3·1 and 3·6.

6 The carbon dioxide gas has been unable to escape If you are not using an orthodox airlock permitting the gas to escape freely, it may be that the gas is going into solution and this could inhibit the yeast. The answer is simply to aerate the wine by pouring it into another container. This enables the carbon dioxide to escape and helps the wine to pick up some free oxygen from the air, with which the yeast cells can make a comeback.

7 *The yeast has reached its limit of alcohol tolerance* Each yeast strain is inhibited by a certain concentration of alcohol. For example, wild yeast ceases to reproduce itself after 4 per cent alcohol has been formed. Bread yeast will remain active up to 13 or 14 per cent alcohol, while some wine yeasts, given perfect circumstances, can ferment up to 18 per cent alcohol. Now, obviously, when these limits of alcohol have been reached in a wine the yeast becomes inhibited. It is not killed nor does it die. Ethyl alcohol only kills yeast in a concentration of 50–70 per cent in an aqueous solution.

When fermentation is completed and the wine racked, a further deposit will be thrown. This deposit includes a number of inhibited but viable yeast cells. Upon further racking the deposit can be used to start a fresh fermentation of a new must, clearly showing that the yeast does not die from alcoholic poisoning – at least at that comparatively low concentration.

Maturation

When fermentation is completely finished the new wine will begin to clear from the top downwards and a thick deposit will be seen at the bottom of the jar. The first racking should now be made, by siphoning the wine into a clean jar and making sure that none of the residue accompanies it. One crushed Campden tablet per six bottles of wine should be added to prevent oxidation and infection if the wine is dry, and two tablets if the wine is sweet. The jar should be topped up with excess wine of the same ferment, with a similar type wine or with a little cold boiled water. It is important that the jar should be well filled and that there is no large air space between the wine and the well-fitting cork. A label should be affixed to describe the wine, and it should be set to mature in a dark place free from vibration and with as even a temperature as possible. The optimum is 10°C.

After 2 months the wine should be looked at again and a further deposit may be seen at the bottom of the jar. The wine will no doubt look much clearer and may even appear bright. Rack again now and top up as before, recorking and labelling before putting the wine back for another three months, when this process should be repeated. The final racking can be made when the wine is bottled.

Too strong an emphasis cannot be placed on this racking. It is during this period that the wine develops its subtle bouquet and flavour and loses the harshness of youth. It mellows. This is the time too, when, according to *Larousse Gastronomique* and repeated experience, the yeast imparts to the wine its own special flavour. The reasons for this are as yet not very clear, but are probably associated with yeast autolysis. Commercial wine is always so racked and this practice of frequent racking is as old as the hills. In addition, frequent rackings help to clear a hazy wine and upon each racking the wine becomes brighter.

There are a few winemakers who are 'crazy' on filtering, and advocate the addition of all sorts of chemicals from nameless bottles, followed by violent stirrings and frequent sloshing through a filter bag set up on a tripod like a witch's cauldron. Have none of this. Almost every wine will clear naturally and of its own accord when it is ready to do so and

Fermentation jar, decanter and glasses

Corking Equipment. Plastic capsules, corker, wires, bottle corks, plastic stopper, bungs, cork stoppers, label and corkscrew

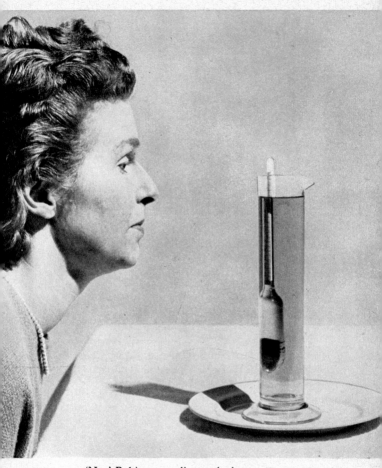

'Nan' Robinson reading an hydrometer

Mashing Equipment. Plastic dustbin holds 4 gallons. Glazed earthenware crock holds 1½ gallons. Home-made press and cloths, filter bag and funnel

aided by simple racking. If it doesn't, there is some good reason for it and the reason should be found.

The most common cause of cloudiness is pectin haze. Tiny particles of cellular material undissolved by the natural pectinase remain suspended in the wine. One can tell in a few moments if this is so by mixing a little methylated spirits with less wine. If jelly-like clots or strings appear then, the haze is due to pectin. The simple cure is to take out some wine from the jar, stir in some pectin-destroying enzyme, stand this in a nice warm place for four days, then pour it back into the jar, which also stands in a warm place, for a day or two. The pectin will then precipitate and the wine can be racked clear.

If after a year, and in spite of the four rackings and a check on pectin haze, your wine has not cleared – and this will be quite unusual – then the wine may be fined. Branded finings are on the market, but care should be taken to buy the best from a reputable firm. Bentonite, gelatine and isinglass are often used and so, too, is egg-white. Four egg-whites well beaten up in a litre of wine will clear as much as 230 litres, so half an egg-white thoroughly beaten into a little wine will clear as much as you are likely to have on hand. As the beaten egg-white slowly sinks to the bottom it takes all the hazy particles with it. If you must 'fine', egg-white can be recommended.

The main objection to filtering and fining is that we don't know what else is removed in the process. A wine that may achieve greatness if left to mature naturally could well be fined and drunk while still mediocre. As a definite policy, then, never filter or fine your wine unless you are forced to – and then do it with great care.

Insufficient storage jars sometimes compel winemakers to

bottle their wine rather sooner than is desirable, but do try not to bottle until the wine is at least clear. There is abundant evidence to show that the wine improves in bulk better than in bottle. Generally, try not to bottle until the wine is nearly a year old. Other considerations apart, it is easier to resist drinking your wine while it is still in bulk than it is once it is bottled. As soon as it is bottled the temptation to try it is overwhelming, and all too often the lot has gone before it has matured.

When bottling time comes, make an absolute point of using only proper wine bottles. Clear glass for white and gold wines and dark green for red wines. The green glass protects the colour of your wine and prevents fading. Each bottle should be punted, that is, with a dent in the bottom. Most restaurants and hotels will gladly give used wine bottles to you. Wash them thoroughly both inside and out and never, never be tempted to add your wine to the little drop in the bottle. Almost for certain this little drop will have oxidized and could spoil your wine. In any case, and if it is still good, the quantity will be too small to affect your wine. Throw it away and start afresh. After washing your bottles, rinse them thoroughly inside and out and stand them upside down to drain for a few minutes.

It is not imperative for the inside of the bottle to be absolutely dry, but it is imperative that it should be absolutely clean. To this end it is well worth while to wash, rinse and drain every wine bottle as soon as it is empty, then when the time comes to fill it, a simple sulphite rinse and drain will be sufficient. Dissolve a few citric acid crystals and one Campden tablet in ·5 litre of cold water and pour this solution from bottle to bottle, turning them upside down to drain afterwards. This solution sterilizes the bottles effectively.

The easiest method of filling the bottles is by siphoning off from a jar. Fill them to 2·5 cm up the neck, so that there is a space of about 2 cm between the wine and the cork when the cork is inserted. Pushing in the cork compresses the air, and unless this little space is left you might push the wine out through the bottom of the bottle ! ! !

Cylindrical corks are best if the wine is to stay long in bottle, but cork stoppers will do admirably for a short while. Cylindrical corks need to be soaked in warm water for a while to soften them, and to be on the safe side a Campden tablet can be dissolved in the water beforehand. As soon as the corks feel soft, they should be dried in a cloth and then soaked for a few minutes in a little of the wine to be bottled.

By placing a thin piece of string or plastic-covered wire in the neck of the bottle it is possible to push the cork right home with the heel of the hand. The string or wire is then withdrawn to the sound of a slight hiss and the cork stays tight. The purpose of the string or wire is to enable some of the air to escape as it is compressed by the cork. This same method is always used with cork stoppers, which should be softened beforehand by the water, but not soaked in wine. The purpose of the wine is to mitigate any flavour from the cork, but used with the stopper it would attract bacteria to the top.

When there are more than half a dozen bottles to be corked at a time it is worth while having and using a corker for the cylindrical corks. This takes the burden out of the work and ensures a good snug fit. The job can be finished neatly with a foil or plastic capsule coloured to match the wine, and a label, plain or fancy just as you please, but at least stating the name and date of the wine. Wine that is to be stored in bottle for more than a few weeks, should be laid on its side so that the cork remains moist. If the cork should dry out, air might be able to enter through the pores of the cork and spoil the wine. Wine that is to stay for only a few weeks in bottle before it is consumed may be stoppered and the bottles stood upright. The cork stoppers can be easily withdrawn by hand and may be washed and used again. Cylindrical corks, on the other hand, have to be withdrawn with the aid of a corkscrew, which damages the cork beyond all further use.

6 How to do it: practice

All the theory of making and maturing wine in general has now been covered, but in this chapter every stage will be described in the making of one particular wine. The wine will be made in two forms, both dry and sweet. The same basic ingredients will be used; the difference will be in the yeasts, in the quantity of sugar and in the length of fermentation. The two wines are made in exactly the same way at first; the difference does not develop until near the end.

Although the ingredients mentioned below are for 6 bottles each of gooseberry hock and gooseberry sauterne, different ingredients may be used in a similar way.

Gooseberry hock

hard green gooseberries	1,250 g
*hock grapejuice concentrate	250 g
sugar	800 g
water (approx)	3·5 litres
acid	nil
tannin	¼ level teaspoon
pectic enzyme	as directed
Campden tablets	
nutrient	
hock yeast	

*Alternatively, 250 g washed and chopped sultanas may be used.

Gooseberry sauterne

ripe golden gooseberries	1,250 g
*sauterne grapejuice concentrate	250 g
sugar	1,000 g
water (approx)	3·5 litres
tartaric acid	2 level teaspoons
tannin	½ level teaspoon
pectic enzyme	as directed
Campden tablets	
nutrient	
sauterne yeast	

*Alternatively, 250 g washed and chopped raisins
may be used.

Before preparing the must, the yeasts should be activated in
separate starter bottles. Two half-size bottles should be sterilized and half-filled with cold boiled water; into them should
go a little acid and nutrient, a dessertspoonful of sugar and
the appropriate yeast. If some fruit juice is available it should
be boiled and used instead of the water. All the ingredients
should be shaken to dissolve them, and the neck of each bottle
should be plugged with cotton wool. Each bottle should be
labelled with the name of the yeast it contains and stood in as
warm a place as possible – 24°C is best. Next day, you should
be able to see plenty of bubbles rising in the bottle, and this is
the time to prepare the must.

Wash the gooseberries after topping and tailing them. If
sultanas or raisins are used these should also be washed and
chopped and added to the gooseberries, and these should be
placed in separate bins. Boil the water and pour it on to the
fruit, then cover the bins and leave to cool.

Crush each berry with your fingers, add 1 crushed Campden

tablet to each bin and as much pectic enzyme as recommended by the manufacturer. (Some preparations are stronger than others and the recommended quantity may be a teaspoonful or a tablespoonful). Cover the bins again and leave them in a warm place for 24 hours. The pectic enzyme will break down the pectin and extract the flavour from the fruit. The Campden tablet will inhibit the growth of micro-organisms.

Next day, add the acid, tannin, grapejuice concentrate, nutrient and activated yeast. Cover the bins again and leave for 4 days, but press down the fruit cap twice daily .

Strain out and press the fruit until it is dry, stir in the sugar, pour the must into fermentation jars, fit airlocks, label with the details of the wine and place the jars in a warm position.

The hock may be allowed to ferment right out and then moved into a cool place for 1 week before racking into a clean jar.

The sauterne has to be watched and the specific gravity checked from time to time. When it has fallen to 1·016, rack the wine into a clean jar and add 2 crushed Campden tablets to terminate the fermentation. Place the jar in a cool position and as soon as a further deposit has formed, rack again, add another Campden tablet, bung tight, label and store.

The hock needs only 1 Campden tablet to prevent oxidation and infection. The labelling is most important since both wines will look alike, although they will taste quite different.

Mature both wines in bulk for 9 months, then have the jars out one at a time and bottle off into clean dark-tinted bottles, corking tightly and labelling carefully. It is always as well to use a number of half-bottles. As you know, wine bottles come in two sizes, the larger holding 75 cl and the smaller 37 cl. On this basis it is possible to fill four large bottles and four half-bottles from one 4·5 litre jar.

The hock-type wine is now almost ready for drinking, as a table wine with roast pork or poultry. It is just possible that the wine will taste a little too dry for your palate, especially if you are not an experienced wine drinker. If this is so, it can be sweetened slightly, bottle by bottle, just before you drink it. At first dissolve only 1 teaspoonful sugar in a little of the wine and then add it to the rest of the bottle. If this is still too dry, try just one more teaspoonful, but do be careful because it is so easy to spoil this fine wine by over-sweetening it.

The sauterne-type wine, being stronger, is likely to take a little longer to mature, maybe another 3–6 months, but then it can be served as a dessert table wine with a meal or during the evening with fruit cake, shortbread or sweet biscuits. It should be treated with respect, since it contains 12 per cent alcohol.

Although the two wines have been made from similar ingredients and basically in the same way, you will find an undisputed difference in flavour, each resembling closely the commercial wine which gave the yeast its name. This is a very good example of the difference that exists between yeasts when used properly. It is also a good example of wine made at home. Both wines will be found delicious if served chilled (10°C), and you will immediately decide to make much larger quantities of them in the future.

All other types of wine may be attempted by the amateur winemaker with success. The most important facts to bear in mind are:

1 to use a good quality yeast of the appropriate variety;
2 to use a sympathetic fruit base; and
3 to follow as nearly as possible the commercial methods for the particular wine.

Sherry is especially popular, and an excellent imitation sherry can be made, especially of the medium sweet and cream varieties. A dry sherry is more difficult to achieve.

Sherry is the only wine that must be fermented and matured in the presence of some air. When fermenting this wine, fill the jar to seven-eighths full or use a larger jar and plug the neck with cotton wool instead of an airlock. The wine must be fed with sugar syrup and fermented to as high a degree of alcohol as is possible. It is essential to use a good sherry yeast with plenty of balanced nutrient and a base such as prunes or Victoria plums, which adopt the sherry flavour admirably. Ferment on the pulp for a few days after removing the stones, then strain and press the fruit and continue fermentation of the wine in a jar for as long as possible. When fermentation finally finishes, the wine should be racked into a clean jar filled to the top, and re-racked every 6 weeks for the first 6 months to ensure the development of the sherry flavour. It needs to be matured for 2 years and may be sweet or dry.

You will have heard of the sherry 'flor', which sometimes develops on the wine when it is made in southern Spain. It is extremely unlikely that your wine will ever develop a sherry flor; the atmosphere here can never be the same as there.

Sherry flor is a strain of sherry yeast which sometimes develops on the wine made in southern Spain, but not always. It does not appear in every cask by any means, but when it does appear in the May following the vintage, it looks like a thick, crinkly, creamy skin. After some time it settles to the bottom of the cask, but reappears on the surface of the wine the following year. The wine in which the flor appears becomes a dry and crisp 'Fino' wine; the wine in which it does not appear becomes an 'Oloroso' and is often sweetened to become a cream sherry. 'Amontillado' is medium sherry, taking its name from the region which makes it best. Sherry is, of course, a fortified wine, and grape spirit is added towards the end of the fermentation to bring the alcoholic content up to at least 18 per cent. It is also a blended wine, one year's vintage always being blended with vintages of a number of other years in selected proportion to ensure the constancy in flavour and style of the wine about to be bottled. This is known as the solera system and costs much money and many years of hard work to produce. Young sherry refreshes old sherry and takes on the flavour and characteristics of the old. At home, a solera system could be built up over the years by applying the same commercial principles. Having made a cask of wine in, say, 1974, three-quarters of it could be bottled in 1975 and the cask filled up with the 1975 vintage of the same blend of wine. In 1976, three-quarters of the cask can again be bottled and the cask again filled up, this time with the 1976 vintage, and so on.

Adding alcohol is not essential, provided the wine is really well fermented. You can sometimes achieve 18 per cent alcohol by fermentation alone.

Sherry yeast available in this country usually has a somewhat sweet flavour, so that even if the wine is fermented down to a specific gravity of 1·000, it is still likely to taste sweetish rather than dry. With this in mind, a sherry yeast can also be used to make a sweet-tasting wine of low alcohol content for table purposes. Beginning with a specific gravity of 1·080 or thereabouts, and fermenting out to dryness, the wine will not be too strong to serve at table, and yet will still have a sweetish flavour.

Sparkling wines always look jolly, and a winemaker with good sparkling wines will be the subject of envy. Again they are not difficult to make if you think of the commercial principles involved. Use a good champagne yeast such as the

Hautville, and a must prepared from a blend of apples and pears. A little extra body should be added in the form of sultanas or grapejuice concentrate. Again not too much sugar, specific gravity 1·080 is plenty. Ferment out, then rack, mature for six months, racking at intervals of two months, and when the wine is quite clear, bottle into champagne bottles. Before corking them, however, make up a solution containing the equivalent of one level teaspoonful of sugar per bottle with a little fermenting champagne yeast from a yeast starter bottle. Add the mixture equally to each bottle, close them with hollow domed plastic stoppers and wire down. Leave this wine for at least six months and store the bottles upside down so that the deposit settles in the hollow dome of the stopper. Before serving, chill the neck of the bottle in some ice and salt until the wine in the stopper is frozen. Remove the stopper with the frozen sediment in it, fit a new stopper, replace the wire fastening and allow the temperature of the wine to increase to 8–10°C.

The chilling retards the expulsion of the carbon dioxide bubbles and they do not fizz too much until the wine is in the glass and warming up. This is a wine well worth making, but do use the strong champagne bottles in case too great a pressure builds up and a thinner bottle bursts.

Aperitif-type wines need to be strong in alcohol, therefore fermented slowly with several additions of sugar. The flavour should be somewhat crisp and slightly bitter, such as is given by Seville oranges, grapefruit, pineapple and so on. While it should not be sweet, it should not be too dry. A sherry yeast will do quite well on the right base and ferment out to dryness.

In general, look critically at the commercial type and apply your knowledge to your own experience.

7 Making the most of your wine

There may be said to be four stages in the life of wine: preparation, fermentation, maturation and consumption. The first three stages have been discussed at some length and now it is the turn of the fourth. Consumption cannot – or rather should not – begin until maturation is complete and the wine quite ready for drinking.

The first and most important factor is that the wine should be suitable for the occasion and the company. To this end you should think carefully before you even start to make wine. Winemaking at home is a long way past the days when dandelion or parsnip wine was made as such and drunk as such without regard to their relationship with the rest of life's food and drink. Today wine should be made for a purpose, as an aperitif, as a table wine, as a dessert wine or even as a liqueur.

Making wine for a particular purpose is all important. Knowing your own eating and drinking tastes means that by careful planning you can provide for all your various wine needs. For example, if you are very fond of a drink before your lunch and dinner, then obviously you need to make a fair supply of aperitif-type wine. If on the other hand you prefer an extra glass of something rich after your meal, then you want a large supply of dessert wine. If your main purpose with your winemaking is to provide a drink to accompany your meals, then you must concentrate on table wine of varying kinds. It is as well to consider your likes and dislikes quite carefully, and then to make an adequate quantity of wine to meet your likes. In addition, it is worth while occasionally to make a small quantity experimentally, to see how you like this wine or that.

Table wines in variety are not difficult to make. Wines to serve the same purpose as claret, sauterne, burgundy and hock can be made simply with just a little care in the choice of a base ingredient and the right yeast. Sparkling wines using a champagne yeast are also delightful. However, without the facilities of freezing the lees in the neck of the bottle and removing them in the commercial manner, it is inevitable that there will be some deposit in the bottle at the moment of serving. Nevertheless, it is possible to pour the wine in such a manner that the deposit is not shaken up and the wine will sparkle beautifully in the glass.

Dessert wines are equally easy to make in variety. Remember that they need to be of good bouquet, full-bodied, rich in taste and strong in alcohol, sweetish, yet with some distinction in character. They should never be insignificant and insipid.

Aperitif wines are perhaps the most difficult for the home winemaker, since nearly all commercial aperitifs have added alcohol, an activity often frowned upon by the wine lover, even though port and sherry fall into this class of fortified wines. And yet splendid wines of an aperitif kind can be produced at home. The object is to achieve as strong a wine as normal fermentation will allow, finished slightly on the sweet side of dry, with good bouquet and flavour without either of them being too pronounced. Without being rich, the wine should be well-bodied and although it should never taste acid, it may be slighly astringent. Such a wine can often be made from grapefruit, oranges (including some Sevilles), pineapples and the like. A sherry yeast is often the one likely to give the best results, but as the sherry yeast frequently finishes with a sweet-ish flavour, it is as well to ferment the wine out to dryness on hydrometer readings and to sweeten slightly, only if necessary.

The future of making good wine at home lies in this making of wine for a specific purpose rather than making up a recipe and accepting whatever comes. There is no need for this. It is just as easy to make what you want as to take what you get. To this end there are an increasing number of us who are turning to professionally made wines for standards. The first fact we learned was that every commercial wine was recommended for a particular purpose. This is the first lesson we can apply to our own wine. The second fact we learned was that the com-mercial wine we could buy was of a relatively even standard. You know pretty well what you are going to get when you order your wine. Our wine, on the other hand, varies widely. Some of it is undoubtedly superior to its commercial equiva-lent, some of it is a long way below. This is more often than not due to making wine to a recipe rather than with skill and knowledge.

If you want to improve your winemaking, taste as much commercial wine as you can and set that as your standard. Taste the wine critically and examine the sugar content, acidity, bouquet, flavour, body, aftertaste, etc. And do the same not only with your own wines but also with the wine made by your friends. Many amateur winemakers belong to clubs and have tasting sessions. When you get the opportunity, taste as many different wines as you can, never accepting more than a dessert-spoonful of any one wine. This is plenty to savour and a mouth-ful to enjoy or discard! If opportunity comes your way, offer to act as a steward to a judge at a wine competition. Your only responsibility is to uncork the bottles and to keep the glasses clean – menial jobs, maybe, but every judge offers the steward a taste and there is no better way of acquiring knowledge of other people's endeavours. You cannot help learning!

The question of the temperature at which wines should be served is one that is often regarded as a connoisseur's foible. It certainly is not. It can make or mar the wine. What is important to remember is that red wines are NOT *ipso facto* served at room temperature and white wines chilled. It is true that red wines often contain more tannin and that they are often richer and stronger than white wines but each wine should be considered on its merits. For example, a parsnip wine that was strong and somewhat heavy, not to say 'heady' would be better served at room temperature as a dessert wine than chilled. On the other hand a mixed summer fruit wine, light and rosé, would probably taste much better at 12°C than at 20°C.

If the wine is light in texture and in alcohol, it can be served cool, and if it is inclined to sweetness then cold – though never less than 8°C. On the other hand, if it is a 'full' wine, pronounced in bouquet and flavour, strong and well-matured, then serve it at room temperature, say 20°C.

Almost every wine made at home, with the possible exception of a sparkling wine, is all the better for being served in a decanter. First, of course, it looks better and the first duty of any wine is to please the eye. Secondly, an hour or two in a decanter – again depending on the age and strength of a wine – enables it to 'breathe'. Dissolved carbon dioxide gas disperses and the comparatively wide surface of wine exposed to the air in the decanter enables subtle esters to develop so that when the wine is poured into a glass it can perform its second duty, to please the nose!

Glasses should invariably be of thin, clear glass. Not so thin that they are fragile to handle, of course, but not so thick that

they look coarse and ugly. They should be completely devoid
of coloured motifs, particularly the clubs, diamonds, hearts and
spades of playing cards, vintage motor cars, bikini-clad beauties
and the like. Apart from spoiling the appearance of the white,
these motifs may be a source of distraction. Etching and cut-
ting is not taboo provided it is not too heavy. A glass is to wine
as a frame is to a picture. Just as the frame, while being seen
should not intrude itself on the picture, so should a glass
enable you to enjoy seeing and smelling the wine without your
being aware of it.

The bowl of the glass should preferably be slightly incurved
at the top so that the rising bouquet can be concentrated rather
than dispersed. The stem and base should be sufficient in
length and size so that the glass can be held safely without the
need to finger the bowl and so mar the view with greasy
imprints.

When washing decanters and glasses, rinse them finally in
cold, clean water and leave them upside down to drain. The
outside should be dried and polished with a good linen cloth.
As soon as your decanters or glasses are emptied they should be
washed and not left for a ring to form. If stains form on the
bottom of a decanter they should be removed with bleach, NOT
shot, chain or a bottle brush, and the decanter then rinsed
thoroughly several times before being upturned to drain.
Abrasive materials only aggravate the position.

Aperitif and dessert wines served to guests not at table are
greatly enhanced in aesthetic pleasure to the eye if they can
be served in polished clear glasses on a silver salver. If your
affluence does not run so high, then at least manage a white
damask-covered tray. The appearance is much enhanced in
these circumstances, while much is lost on a coloured wood,
plastic or fancy tray.

Good wine deserves the accompaniment of good food and different wines appear to go better with some foods than with others. There is no fixed relationship, and this being a free world you can drink whatever wine you like with whatever food you like. Experience shows, however, that in the main, light wines are best with light foods and fuller wines with heavier and richer foods. Dry wines are often better with fatty foods, while slightly sweet wines are better with non-meat dishes. Puddings almost always need a sweet wine. Cheese happily accompanies all wines.

The late Maurice Healy had a dictum to the effect to serve your best wines to your best friends on your great occasions, and to serve your other wine on other days. This question of company is very important. It is a waste of good wine to serve it to an unappreciative guest, and there is never enough to waste! On the other hand, a range of carefully selected wines served in accompaniment with well-prepared food to your dearest friends is always an event of heightened pleasure. Whether they are winemakers or not, however, it is always as well only to offer a small portion of wine at first. It is a far happier thing to hear them ask for more than to see them squirming as they surreptitiously seek somewhere to surrender their wine. The greatest wine connoisseurs of today say that it takes thirty years to cultivate a good palate. Maybe your friends are not yet as far along the road as you, maybe they are somewhat farther. Be modest about your wine. Let it speak for itself. Never fill a guest's glass and say, 'I think this is rather good.' It might be the end of what could have become a wonderful friendship. Instead, offer perhaps only a tasting sip and invite them to 'try this!' If it is really good, it won't need you to say so. If it isn't to your guest's palate you will be the more respected for not forcing it upon him.

In this connection it is important to remember never to fill a glass more than two-thirds full in any circumstances. There are four good reasons for this:

1 It looks much more pleasing to the eye.
2 It enables the bouquet to collect on top of the wine and yet to remain within the glass.
3 It saves the wine from being spilled when the glass is moved.
4 It gives your guest the opportunity to accept a second glass.

In this chapter there is yet another topic which will enable you to make the most of your wine, and that is the use of wine in cooking.

Far too many English housewives seem afraid to use wine in everyday cooking. Possibly it is because it is expensive to buy wine for cooking and if this is so, they should be especially glad to have so much excellent inexpensive wine in the house. Our wine made at home is perhaps better for cooking than is commercial wine. Generally speaking, it is stronger in both flavour and alcohol than commercial wine, and this seems to be advantageous.

This is not a 'How to Cook with Wine' book, but a few examples may be just what you need to set you off into another new interest.

Stewed apples, indeed all fruit, are much improved if you use a glassful of white wine instead of water when cooking them.

Strawberries develop a flavour undreamed of if after stalking, rinsing, draining and sugaring them, you pour over them one glassful of red wine and leave for two hours in the bottom of the refrigerator.

Fresh pineapple becomes a dish from the Ritz if it is peeled, cut into pieces and steeped in white wine for a few hours.

Dried prunes or apricots stacked in a Kilner jar and covered with wine – red or white – then sealed and left for six months, become a delicacy that can ruin your figure, they are so tempting.

Whiting, of all fish, baked in a white wine and served with a sauce made from the liquor, is a dish fit for a queen.

Kipper fillets marinaded in dry red wine for twenty-four hours, then strained and served with watercress become the poor man's smoked salmon!

Breasts of lamb, boned and cut small, then braised with a little onion and mushroom in half a bottle of red wine and served with a thick sauce made from the liquor, is another inexpensive dish for which the rich pay dearly.

Always add white wine to a roasting fowl and pour a glass of red wine over the roast beef or lamb a few minutes before taking it from the oven. Make sure that you use the stock for gravy.

There is no end to the variety of uses to which you can put your wine. As a general guide, use wine light in alcohol and delicate in flavour for marinading, and stronger, coarser wines for actual cooking. Do not worry about the children, for in cooking much of the alcohol is driven off by the heat.

8 What went wrong

Fortunately, if it is well made, wine suffers from relatively few ailments and these can nearly always be avoided by common sense and simple hygiene. By far the most common ailment, though in fact it rarely happens more than once in a lifetime, is infection by the vinegar bacillus – *Mycoderma aceti*. It is caused by inadequate covering of the must during mashing or, at some stage, leaving the fermenting wine exposed too long to the air. As a result the vinegar bug, floating invisibly in the air, falls on to the must or wine, finds this an excellent source of food, multiplies very rapidly and turns the must or wine into vinegar. When this has happened there is no known way of turning it back to wine. If you have occasion to use so much vinegar then it is perfectly good for all vinegar purposes. Boil it for five minutes, pour it into sterilized bottles and seal them immediately. If you do not want the vinegar, then pour it down the drain and flush it away, thoroughly washing and sterilizing the vessel that contained it.

It is also possible to ruin wine by racking it at the same time as you are pickling onions or making chutney. Wine and vinegar just do not go together and should always be kept well apart. In fact, no highly flavoured or spiced food or anything strong-smelling, such as paraffin, petrol, creosote, etc., should be stored near wine, either in the making or in the maturing. Even in a cask, wine would tend to absorb a horrible smell, but the remedy is simple common sense, when once you know.

At the risk of being boring then, the dictum is repeated : *at all times keep must and wine well covered and away from strong-smelling neighbours.*

Another ailment called 'casse' or 'break' is caused by particles of iron or copper dissolving in the wine. Obviously this cannot occur if the wine is never allowed to come into contact with such metals or indeed any metal. It is rarely seen today, but should it ever happen to you it is best to throw the wine away and start again.

Almost the only other ailment that you are ever likely to come across is ropiness. This is caused by bacilli which string together to form 'ropes' in the wine. On pouring such a wine it has a thick and oily appearance, although it smells and tastes all right. The remedy is to crush 2 Campden tablets per gallon and stir them into the wine. Stir very thoroughly with a beating action to break up the chains, leave it for a few days for the precipitate to settle and then rack off the clear wine into a fresh jar.

Failure to clear has already been mentioned. It is always best to leave a wine to clear naturally, even if this takes a year and a number of rackings to achieve. If it is still 'veiled' or hazy there are a number of branded wine finings or clarificants, as they are called, available to help you. Many secret formulae are marketed. Professional winemakers have recourse to beaten white of egg when necessary, and this is recommended because it is so readily available, is so cheap and is most efficient. Half a white of an egg well beaten into a half-bottle of wine will clear 25 litres in a matter of days. But do not be in a hurry to clear your wine. The best quality wine is produced by natural clearing and you should only turn to other means as a last resource.

It is always so much easier to prevent things going wrong than it is to correct them. To this end always keep your wine-making equipment clean. It is not necessary to go to the lengths of laboratory sterilization, but ordinary kitchen hygiene should be scrupulously followed. Whenever you are finished with a piece of equipment, wooden spoon, rubber tube, mashing vessel, airlock or what you will, wash it in hot water at once. Dry it and then put it away in a clean place. Before you use it again rinse it in hot water to remove any loose dust and germs. If you haven't used it for some months then wash it thoroughly and soak it for a few minutes in a bottle of water in which 1 Campden tablet has been dissolved.

Never put bottles or jars or corks away dirty or wet. Wash them immediately after use and drain them dry. Some wine-makers plug the necks of their jars with cotton wool while in store unused, but this is only necessary if they are not going to be used for quite a while. Vessels that you are using every few weeks do not need this as long as they are put away dry. If they are put away wet, the water goes musty and the bottle or jar develops an unpleasant smell. Incidentally the best way to tell whether a bottle, jar or cask is suitable to contain wine is to smell it. If you can smell anything at all, then it is not fit and must be cleaned again. A good long bottle brush is an invaluable aid in cleaning bottles and jars and always make sure that you give an extra twist under the shoulder!

In spite of every effort to make a good wine, it sometimes happens that for reasons over which you may not have any control, the wine fails to be a vintage wine and indeed may not even be particularly palatable. A bad summer can cause this, poor quality fruit, or fruit specially high in acid or tannin and so on, with many other reasons yet unknown to us. Provided the wine is sound and not vinegarish, do not throw it away, but blend it.

Blending is as old as winemaking itself. From the very beginning all sorts of herbs, spices, fruits and honey have been added to make wine palatable. The position commercially is not much different. Sometimes the wine is wonderful, sometimes the vigneron is ashamed of it. Different wines are blended together, some have grape sugar added to them, some have alcohol added. The wine of one year is blended with another, but always blending, blending, blending to achieve an acceptable wine. Some wines such as sherry are always blended, variety with variety and year with year, the young refreshing the old, the old giving flavour and character to the young.

In the amateur winemaking movement there are still many who think you should be able to make a vintage wine every time and often regard every wine they make as vintage when, in fact, it should be blended. Three hundred years or so ago it was the custom among many wine merchants of the day to blend one hogshead of grape wine imported from the Continent with three hogsheads of fruit wine made at home, the blend was then sold as Continental wine at a nice profit. Experience in blending over many years has shown that wine made from concentrated grapejuice, while not often very acceptable by itself does add considerable virtues to fruit wine and you are strongly recommended to try this for yourself.

In blending wine together it is not necessary to keep red and white wine separate, but it is important to taste each wine carefully and try to decide what it is that makes that wine just not quite right. The wines should then be blended, with these thoughts in mind. For example, it would not be wise to blend only excessively sharp or acid wines together, nor those which are all astringent. Mix in some of each wine, including those that are too sweet, any which have not fallen bright, some, but not too much, of any with an overpowering flavour – an indication that you have used too much of the base ingredient. Wherever possible include one still fermenting. A really worthwhile practice is to decide in advance which wines you intend to blend and how much of each and the size of your container and then, before blending them, to start a gallon of grape-concentrate wine.

This concentrate can be bought from all the major suppliers listed in the appendix on page 168, in quantities from 1 kg to 6 kg. Recipes come with each container, but basically for a dry wine you simply add water equivalent to three times your quantity of concentrate and yeast. For sweeter wines you just reduce the quantity of water. For blending purposes always make up a dry wine, i.e. 1 kg of concentrate will make up 6 bottles of wine. When the fermentation has been going on for about two weeks, blend this in with your chosen wines and only lightly bung your cask, or if you are using a jar, plug the neck with cotton wool or cover it with a piece of sheet polythene held down by a rubber band. Leave your blend in the warm for a while and it is often useful to add a little extra yeast energizer or booster such as Tronozymol at this stage. All the wines will now be integrated through the fermentation. A large polythene bin is especially useful for blending, and if you are making a good deal of wine a 50 litre blending bin is an excellent investment. If you haven't such a large bin the wines must be mixed together as best you can and then poured into jars plugged with cotton wool or fitted with airlocks.

Fermentation may go on for another two, three or four weeks, but when it is finished the wine will fall bright and after three or four months should be racked and stored again for at least another three or four months when it may be bottled and set out for use. There is no doubt at all that you will be quite amazed at the quality of this blended wine. Your wine will have taken on the good attributes of each of the constituent wines which will have lost their poorer quality.

If there is some science in winemaking there is certainly art in blending and experience, and knowledge of winemaking in general will be found most helpful. Never be afraid to try. It is a far better risk to blend your unsatisfactory wines than to serve them as they are. There is nothing to be ashamed of in making a non-vintage wine. This happens at times to the greatest vignerons in the world and we can never aspire to such heights as this, based very often on many generations of knowledge and experience and a lifetime spent in the work aided by chemists and experts. Do try blending, then, and when you have produced, as you will do, an excellent wine as the result, you can have another kind of pleasure in making up a suitable name for your wine.

The advantages of storing wine in casks were mentioned earlier on and the best winemakers would agree that every wine benefits from at least six months in a cask. As a result, more and more casks are coming on to the market. The minimum size worth buying holds 30 bottles but one that will hold 50 bottles is better still. Do not be tempted to buy an old vinegar barrel cheaply, unless you intend to saw it in halves for the garden; it can never be perfectly cleansed and it will always turn your wine sour. The vinegar bacilli get deep into the pores of the staves. Far better to buy one of the reconditioned wine casks available from reputable wine equipment suppliers.

When your cask comes, remove the iron rings one at a time and paint them with anti-rust paint. Replace them and drive them tightly home. Next soak the cask in cold water for forty-eight hours, for it will have arrived dry and will leak badly. After soaking you will find that the staves and the end boards have swollen and made a nice watertight fit. Now you can begin to clean it. Mix up 100 g of common washing soda in 4 litres of boiling water, pour it into the bung-hole and replace the bung. It is assumed that there is a cork in the tap-hole and that there are no loose pieces of cork or bung inside the cask. For the next half-hour, slowly roll the cask from side to side and from end to end. Small children regard this as great fun! Remove the bung and drain out the liquid, then rinse with some more hot water. Fluotone Jaquemin is another excellent cleanser; so, too, is Chempro.

The next step is to mix up a good teaspoonful of citric acid with 4 Campden tablets in a litre of water, pour this into the cask, bung tightly and renew the slow rolling and pitching process. It is obviously imperative to make absolutely certain that the liquid covers every nook and cranny of the inside of the cask. After your stint is over, empty the cask, rinse in hot water and allow to cool. When the cask smells sweet take half a bottle of any sound wine you can spare, pour it into the cask, bung again and repeat the slow rolling and pitching. This imparts a sweet and wholesome smell to the cask. Like the previous cleansing agents, however, it has to be poured away and the cask drained. But it is now ready for your first wine and you can use it safely and with confidence. Use a tight-fitting bung and bang on the staves to remove it. Do not use a screwdriver or the like in case you ruin the shape of the hole. It is not a good thing to leave the cask empty when not in use.

Fill it with boiling water and when cool add 1 Campden tablet and 1 teaspoonful of citric acid per 6 bottles. Every 2 or 3 months empty, rinse and refill as before. But, better still, keep it full of maturing wine and as soon as one wine comes out, wash the cask and put another wine in.

9 Clubs and competitions

Winemaking clubs exist in every town and many villages. The names and addresses of the Secretaries change in most years and so it is obviously not practical to include them. If you wish to contact the one in your area, the local Council Office, Post Office, Library or Citizen's Advice Bureau can often help. If having tried these and other ideas of your own you are still unsuccessful, it is possible that the editors of the monthly journals *The Amateur Winemaker* and *The Home Brewer and Winemaker* can supply the information. Enclose a stamped, addressed envelope for the reply.

It was at Andover that the first Winemakers' Circle, as it is called there, was formed in the early spring of 1954. Within a few months, and without knowledge of the others, Winemakers' Clubs were also formed at Cheltenham and Welwyn Garden City. Slowly at first, other Circles started, until in 1957 Mr C. J. J. Berry started a monthly magazine which he called *The Amateur Winemaker*. The circulation soon soared and the Clubs began to form more quickly as a result of being able to get in touch with each other. It is evident that a great many people had been making wine in isolation for some time and more were most anxious to meet other winemakers, to taste their wines and to exchange experiences.

On Whit Monday 1959 the first Conference of Amateur Winemakers was held at Andover, and a second was held in

Bournemouth in 1960. In October of that year twenty-two representatives of twenty-two clubs met in Andover and formed a Committee to organize the Amateur Winemakers' National Conference and Show, which was held at Harrow in June 1961.

After the tax on home-made beer was repealed in 1963, classes for beer were subsequently included in the show. The National Association of Wine and Beer Makers now includes individual members as well as associated clubs and regional federations of clubs. The latter each hold their own annual show, many of which are as big as the early Nationals.

The National Competition attracts some four thousand bottles of wine and beer spread over forty-odd different classes and it is a wonderful sight to behold. Throughout the country local competitions of up to several hundred bottles are held annually and nearly every club has its own private competition for club members. As a result the standard of presentation has almost universally achieved professional commercial standards. The quality of the wines naturally varies somewhat, but the best are often superior to many commercial wines on sale in this country at high prices. They are made with tremendous love, knowledge and care.

The need to have an authoritative body of efficient judges was seen in 1962 and by the 1963 Show the Amateur Winemakers National Guild of Judges was formed. Adjudication practices were standardized, a Handbook was published and examinations were organized. Membership to the Guild can only be obtained by passing at one time the 3 parts of the examination. One is on the theory of making wine, one is on the principles of adjudication and the third is a practical test of placing a selection of wines in the same order as a panel of Judges.

In the clubs, which usually meet monthly, there is frequently a spirit of fellowship unsurpassed in other organizations. Most clubs have to restrict their membership, so that the members can really know each other. Lectures are given by club members and visiting lecturers on varying aspects of winemaking, sometimes representatives of the commercial wine firms visit to talk about sherry, port or the like.

Every now and again there are tasting sessions in which every member is able to taste the same group of wines and to compare his opinions with those of others. There are, too, social evenings and outings which all contribute to the pleasure of club membership.

If there is no club in your area you will find that a letter to the local paper, asking other winemakers to get into touch with you will produce some remarkable results and you will have a flourishing membership before you know where you are!

One of the most important advantages of being a member of a club is that someone appointed as a supplies officer is able to purchase in bulk for the club, stocks of corks, yeasts, nutrients, airlocks, brushes, hydrometers, raisins, dried elderberries, dried rosehip shells, etc., etc., etc. This enables members to buy their ingredients at a time and place convenient to them and in quantities that would be uneconomic for them to order by post. The small membership fee to pay for the hire of the hall, lecturers' expenses, etc., is soon recouped by members buying their ingredients and equipment through the club instead of by post.

If you have not previously entered a wine competition there are a few small points to watch. In the first place, read the rules carefully and make sure that you follow them to the letter. Consider the wines that you have available and decide which of them are suitable for the various classes. About a week or ten days before the date for entry, set out those bottles you intend to enter and put temporary labels on them. The day before taking the bottles to the show, transfer the wine to selected clear glass punted wine bottles of the kind that hold 75 cl. Sometimes the figure 75 is embossed on the punt of the bottles. These competition bottles should be given a special wash in warm water and then rinsed in cold, up-ended and drained dry. The outside should be wiped with a clean glass-cloth and polished. Examine it to ensure that there are no blemishes on the glass, or chips out of the neck or base. If there are, reject the bottle and find a perfect one.

When the bottle is clean and dry fill it with the selected wine so that the top of the wine is about 2 cm up the neck. Use a new cork stopper which has been washed, soaked and dried, push it well in and label the bottle precisely in accord-ance with the rules. For example, if a label has to be affixed 3 cm from the bottom then measure 3 cm with a ruler – do not just guess! You will see by examining the bottle that there are two seams where the two halves of these mass-moulded bottles are fused together. Labels should *always* be stuck between these two seams, equidistant from both of them and never on any account across one of them.

Finally, hold the bottle of wine up to a good light and give a last examination to the wine to make quite certain that no minute particles of any kind can be seen floating. If there is the least bit you must strain it out. Having made quite sure that with infinite pains you have achieved perfection, give the bottle a last polish to remove any fingerprints and wrap it in tissue paper and take it to the Entry Secretary.

If ever you get the opportunity, try to act as steward to a judge for a competition in which you have no entries. Your duties will include drawing corks, rinsing glasses, replacing corks, returning bottles to their proper place on the stand and generally helping the judge in any other way you can. If you are keen to learn, the judge may allow you to taste the different wines and tell you what he or she thinks of them. These remarks you can compare with your own observations and you will thus rapidly achieve a standard by which you can subsequently judge your own wines. It is an excellent idea to try to write a brief comment on each wine, mentioning obvious faults or qualities and whether you think it is good, bad or indifferent.

The Judge awards marks as follows:

 2 for Presentation, deducting for poor labelling, poor cork, imperfect bottle and under- or over-filled.
 4 for Clarity and Colour, deducting for sediment or pieces of floating debris, haze, however faint, tawniness in a red wine or brown in a white or golden wine, or for the wrong shade of rosé which should be a pretty pink.
 4 for Bouquet, deducting for lack of vinosity or fruitiness, for lack of depth or quality and for any unpleasant smell.
20 for Flavour and Quality according to its class. Marks are deducted if the wine is too sweet or too dry, too acid, too strong in alcohol or flavour, if it is oxidised, unless in such a class, if it suffers from any infection or imperfection in fermentation or maturation.

A total of 30 marks for perfection and therefore never awarded. Winning wines obtain 24 to 26 marks, scoring 2 and 4 in the first two sections and perhaps 3 and 16 in the second two sections.

It is also a tremendous help in achieving a standard by which you judge wines if you take every opportunity you can to taste as many commercial wines as possible. Approach them critically, first studying their appearance, brilliance and colour, then their bouquet and finally their flavour split between 'greeting' or first taste and 'farewell' or aftertaste, when the wine has gone down. Mentally look out for sweetness which you can taste on the top of the tongue, acidity which you will feel on the sides of the tongue towards the tip and bitterness which you taste on the sides towards the back. The three should blend into a smooth whole and no one should predominate. In between each wine, clear your palate with a dry biscuit or piece of cheese – Caerphilly cheese is excellent for this purpose – and try to approach each wine as though it were the first of the day, forgetting for a moment all that have gone before.

Always drink critically, set your standards as high as possible and as your wines the more frequently approach your standard, then raise your standard nearer to perfection.

You should never attempt to judge wine if you have a cold or are suffering from catarrh, if you have indigestion or if you are worried, nor if you have scalded your tongue with hot tea or the like. Your palate will be most acute when you are in good health, both in mind and in body. A placid, unhurried approach enables you to search carefully for all the qualities and any defects there may be in the wine in your glass.

10 Other than wine

Mead

Cave paintings exist which depict Paleolithic Man gathering honey from a hive of bees. This is so far back in history that the dried husks of gourds were used as bowls because clay pots had not yet been invented! Poor old *Homo sapiens*, living on crudely roasted meat and wild berries, must have rejoiced at the thought of some honey diluted with water. One wonders how soon he discovered that, left for a few days, it would begin to ferment, and one can imagine the pleasure obtained from the first rough mead, cloudy and still with the prickle of fermentation yet containing enough alcohol to make him merry. All this was 12,000 years ago.

As knowledge and facilities slowly increased by experience and experiment, flavourings of wild herbs were added and the mead was kept long enough to mature. Two or three thousand years ago, different fruit juices were mixed with the must by way of variation and then, only some hundreds of years ago, spices too were added – such as ginger, clove and the like. And yet, although thousands of years of history had gone into the making of mead, wine made from fermented grapejuice from Greece, then France and later Spain and Portugal supplanted it.

There are, of course, many different kinds of honey: light

and dark, thin and thick, and the flavour will much depend
upon the kind of flowers visited by the bees. There are subtle
differences between clover honey, heather honey, fruit-blossom
honey, garden-flower honey and so on. In spite of these
nuances of flavour the chemical composition of honey remains
fairly constant at 77 per cent sugar, $17\frac{1}{2}$ per cent water and
the balance made of salts of iron, phosphorus, lime, sodium,
potassium, sulphur and manganese, with traces, too, of citric,
formic, malic, succinic and amino acids, dextrin, pollen, oils,
gums, waxes, fats, yeasts, enzymes, vitamins, albumen, protein
and ash. The quantities, though minute, will obviously vary
from honey to honey.

The process of preparation is simply to bring the honey
slowly to the boil in at least an equal amount of water and to
simmer it gently for a quarter of an hour or so till the impurities rise to the surface as a scum which you skim off and
throw away. Three or four pounds of honey will be needed to
make 6 bottles of mead, depending upon whether you want a
dry mead, not too strongly flavoured or one that is sweeter and
stronger both in alcohol and flavour. The light honey is to be
preferred to the dark, which imparts too pronounced a flavour.

Honey is deficient in acid, tannin and nutrient, and these
should not be forgotten when making mead. 15 g of a mixture
of citric and tartaric acid, 1 teaspoonful of tannin and twice
the nutrient necessary for wine. Strictly speaking any other
ingredients apart from yeast, make your mead something other
than mead. Mead containing spices for example is called
'methaglyn' – a Celtic word. And yet the addition of just a
little ginger sharpens the flavour without altering it. A variety
of yeasts can be used, such as sherry, sauterne, champagne and
the like, but a special honey yeast – maury – seems to give a
better flavour to the mead than the others.

Fermentation is carried on in the same way as wine, though frequently it lasts much longer, 6 months or so. It is important to keep the mead in a warm and even temperature the whole time, and this may well be during all the winter months. When fermentation is finished the mead needs to be racked and stored for as long as possible – 2 years and upwards for strong sweet meads.

Dry mead may be served at table with, for example, chicken; sweet mead may be drunk as a dessert wine. The following recipes each make 6 bottles of mead.

Dry mead
1·5 kg white honey
3·5 litres water
15 g acid blend
1 tsp tannin
maury yeast and nutrient

Sparkling mead
1·5 kg white honey
3·5 litres water
15 g acid blend
1 tsp tannin
champagne yeast
and nutrient

Sac or sweet mead
2 kg white honey
225 g white sugar
3 litres water
26 g acid blend
1 tsp tannin
maury
or
sherry yeast and nutrient

After racking this mead when it is bright, bottle in champagne bottles and prime with a teaspoonful of sugar and a teaspoonful of active champagne yeast before sealing with hollow domed plastic stoppers, wired down. Leave for 12 months, disgorge the sediment and serve chilled.

Methaglyn (spiced mead)
2 kg white honey
200 g demerara sugar
3 litres water
20 g acid blend
1 tsp tannin
15 g root ginger and 6 cloves
a grating of nutmeg or cinnamon, to your palate
maury yeast and nutrient

This wine should be served sweet and free from chill. It is not very pleasant when served dry and cold.

Sir Kenelm Digbie's recipe, 1669
1 measure of honey to 3 of water
Boil gently till 1 measure is boiled away.
Take a garni of violet leaves, strawberry leaves, sorrell, rosemary, balme, hart's tongue, liverwort, thyme and red sage. And simmer the honey again for 1 hour. Remove the garni and add cloves, nutmeg and ginger to taste. Add some Blue raisins of the Sun and some yeast of beer or leaven of bread, cover with a thick cloth during fermentation and when finished strain into a storage jar till it clears, then bottle and mature for 2 years.

Pyment is made from honey and grapes. Honey can be used in place of sugar when making grape wine, or some crushed fresh grapes or grapejuice concentrate can be added to a mead must. Alternatively, dried grapes – raisins or sultanas – can be used. 450 g honey replaces 340 g sugar. 500 g raisins or sultanas is equivalent to 2 kg of fresh grapes.

Hypocras is made from spiced grape wine and honey. Spices

may be of your choice; clove, ginger, nutmeg, rosemary, etc., etc., etc., but use them very sparingly. Grapejuice concentrate or raisins could be added to methaglyn.

Cyser is made from honey and apples. The honey could replace some of the sugar in an apple wine, or 1 kg crushed apples could be included when making 6 bottles of sweet mead must.

Melomel is made from honey and mixed fruits. Add 500 g mixed summer fruits to a sweet mead (omit the acid) or replace with honey some of the sugar in mixed-fruit wine.

Ale

Although not as ancient a drink as mead, ale was made and drunk in this country long before the Romans came. At that time it was just a fermented liquor made from a cereal mash, barley, wheat or rye was used. Flavours were sometimes varied with different herbs, and nettle was quite the most popular for many centuries. The Romans who gave so much to our civilization also brought us the hop, though our forebears were slow to welcome it. As a result ale continued to be made for many more centuries and when hops were added it was called beer.

Through the ages, the malting of barley, which is now always used for beer, has been brought to a very fine art and today malting is a very specialized activity carried on near the farms where the barley is grown. The barley is soaked with water and maintained at a precise humidity in a constant and pre-selected temperature for a specified number of days and hours so that a hairlike root called a plumule appears. In this simple but minutely controlled process an enzyme called diastase converts the starch in the grain of barley into a sugar

Other than wine   103

called maltose. The malt is then roasted. If it is intended for pale ale or bitter beer, the roasting is light. For old ale and medium-coloured beers the malt is roasted for a little longer. For stout and black beers the malt is roasted until it is dark brown. The quality of the barley and therefore the malt varies from district to district and from year to year causing subtle differences in the flavour of the beer, though they are not usually discernible to any but the connoisseur.

The quality of the water is very important, too, and some places with water containing gypsum, such as Burton-on-Trent, are famous for their light ales, while others with softer water, such as Dublin, are famous for stout. Many factors affect the flavour of beer, but water is perhaps the most important. The quality and quantity of the malt used and the quality and quantity of the hops used are, of course, the other major factors.

The making is simplicity itself and the ingredients are readily available. All the major suppliers listed in Appendix 3 sell everything you could wish for, but all you really need for a trial brew of beer is a can of extract of malt and hop oils.

The cans of prepared malt extract are available in all the known beer styles: mild, bitter, brown, stout, lager and their variations. They make up into 9, 13, 18 or 22 litres. Yeast and finings are often supplied, and all that is required is some sugar and water. Detailed and simple step-by-step instructions are provided with each kit. The resultant beer is similar in style to commercial beer but can be easily improved by reducing the quantity of water by 15 per cent.

A stone jar or plastic bucket, or a polythene bin is needed for fermenting the beer and it is absolutely essential to have some proper beer bottles in which to mature the beer. Corks are useless with beer. They admit enough air to cause a scum of yeast and bacteria to appear on top of the beer, which goes flat and insipid. With screw stoppers or crown caps a foamy 'head' can be obtained, and the beer poured out full of life and flavour.

A simple basic recipe for an all-purpose beer, using malt extract and hops, is as follows:

1 kg extract of malt
500 g demerara sugar
50 g dried hops
10 litres water
beer yeast

First warm the jar of malt by standing it near the kitchen boiler, or in some hot water, for 10 minutes after opening the can. The malt then pours out quickly and cleanly into the fermentation vessel. Add the sugar and 1 litre of tepid water, and stir till all is dissolved.

Meanwhile, put seven-eighths of the hops into a clean muslin bag or washed nylon stocking, place this in a saucepan of water with 1 litre of water and boil for 10 minutes. Strain this liquor on to the wort in the bucket and repeat the process twice more. The remainder of the hops should now be placed in a muslin bag or the like and added to the wort, then top up with cold water. Cover the vessel to keep out the dust, and when cool add an activated beer yeast. In a short while the yeast will be working as a creamy head. A cover should be left over the vessel to keep out the dust, but fermentation is so vigorous that an airlock is neither necessary nor desirable.

In a day or so the yeast head will contain obvious impurities and these should be removed with a spoon and thrown away. Leave the beer to ferment for at least a week, during which time the specific gravity will have fallen from about 1·036 to

1·004. This is called attenuation. When no more activity occurs, siphon off the beer into clean beer bottles to within about 5 cm from the bottom of the screw top. Not more than one level teaspoonful of sugar should now be added to each pint bottle and the stopper screwed down very tightly.

This addition of sugar, known as priming, must not be overdone. If you succumb to the temptation to add too much priming, so much carbon dioxide will be formed in the second fermentation that either the bottle will burst or there will be such a rush of gas when you release the screw that it will be quite impossible to pour any beer into a glass. On the other hand, failure to add any priming will leave the beer flat and lifeless, insipid and unacceptable as a thirst-quenching drink.

With the right amount of priming the beer will fall bright after 10 days and can be poured gently down the inside slope of the tumbler or beer mug forming a foamy head and a constant sparkle of bubbles, which give that slight prickle to the tongue to denote a fresh and lively beer.

When filling two glasses from the same bottle the second glass should be followed on from the first without the bottle being tilted back or up. It is not possible at home to produce a bottled beer that has no sediment. A sediment can be obtained that stays firm enough to pour out nearly all the beer, but if the bottle is not held firmly and evenly the sediment is stirred up by the resurging beer and the remainder becomes cloudy and tastes yeasty.

Variations of this basic recipe can be made at your own will, to suit your palate. If you live in a soft-water area and wish to make a bitter beer you need to add a packet of hardening salts to your wort. These are obtainable from the suppliers listed. For darker ales you should add 25–50 g of black malt grains when boiling the hops, depending on how strongly flavoured you like your beer. The quantity of hops can also be varied from 30 g up to 100 g to the 10 litres. A number of variations are given, but you can try many of your own. The one already given is, however, proved by thousands of people over many years to be the most popular.

A particularly delicious variation is Cock Ale, made in the manner already described but with pieces of cooked chicken and crushed bones soaked overnight in half a bottle of strong white wine and then all added to the fermenting wort. Attenuation takes up to a week longer and after bottling and priming, this strong ale should be matured for at least 3 weeks. It is a most nourishing and finely flavoured, almost liqueur-type beer. You must certainly try it.

Bitter beer
1 kg malt extract
500 g white sugar
75 g hops
10 g hardening salts
beer yeast
10 litres water

Strong ale
1 kg malt extract
1 kg demerara sugar
75 g hops
beer yeast
10 litres water

Stout
1 kg malt extract
250 g black malt grains
500 g demerara sugar

Mild ale
1 kg malt extract
40 g hops
beer yeast
10 litres water

Brown ale
1 kg malt extract
100 g black malt grains
50 g hops
500 g demerara sugar
1 level tsp table salt
beer yeast
10 litres water

Milk stout
1 kg malt extract
200 g black malt grains
500 g demerara sugar

50 g hops
1 level tsp table salt
stout yeast
10 litres soft water

50 g hops
250 g lactose
1 level tsp table salt
stout yeast
10 litres soft water

Ginger beer
50 g bruised root ginger
1 kg sugar
9 litres water
4 lemons
15 g cream of tartar
1 level tsp granulated yeast

Thinly peel the lemons. Remove and discard the white pit, then cut them into thin wafers. Break up and crush the root ginger, add the sugar and cream of tartar and pour on the boiling water, stirring well. Cover with a thick cloth and when cool add an active yeast. Re-cover and leave for 2 days. Skim off the yeast, strain out the ginger and lemon and bottle in screw-top bottles for 3 days. Serve cold.

Recipes

Introduction

In the pages that follow you will find more than a hundred recipes, in all of which certain words are used regularly. They have already been fully described in the text, but the meaning is given again for the sake of easy reference.

Yeast Most recipes suggest a variety of wine yeast that will impart the best flavour and an appropriate alcohol content to the wine, to be made from the ingredients enumerated. But it does not follow that this yeast only must be used. You may use *any* yeast of your choice. A general purpose wine yeast may always be substituted if you prefer.

The yeast should, however, always be prepared in a starter bottle as described on pages 56–7 and added to the must when it is thoroughly reactivated.

Nutrient Every recipe recommends the addition of yeast nutrient. Use as much as is recommended by the manufacturer. But never omit it.

Pectic enzyme Certain recipes recommend the addition of a pectin-destroying enzyme to the must. This is essential for fruit wines and should not be omitted. Its use not only assists in obtaining a clear wine, but also assists in obtaining the greatest possible extract of flavour from the fruit. Use as much as is recommended by the manufacturer. The quantity varies with the quality.

Campden Tablets These little tablets, so widely used in fruit preservation, are very cheap and should be added to sterilize the must as a matter of habit. Simply crush 1 tablet per 4·5 litres and add the crystals to the must when cool, so that the sulphur dioxide given off can kill any wild yeasts and bacteria that may be present. Add yeast 24 hours later – never at the same time.

Sugar This can be added in syrup or crystal form or invert sugar may be used instead, in which case add a further 20 per cent to allow for the water content of invert sugar.

Acid A blend of citric, tartaric and malic acids is recommended and is called acid blend, but any one of the acids may be used if you prefer. Alternatively, the thinly peeled rind of lemons and their expressed juice may be used. The juice of 4 large lemons is approximately equal to 25 g of acid crystals.

Fermentation The recipes usually only go as far as the addition of the yeast. Fermentation should be carried out as already recommended. For a dry wine, suitable for the table, no additional sugar should be added. For strong wines to be used for aperitif or dessert purposes, small doses of sugar may be added towards the end of fermentation so as to prolong it and enable the yeast to produce the highest quantity of alcohol. When fermentation is finished add sufficient sugar to your taste.

Racking The wine should always be removed from the lees as soon as fermentation is finished and again as soon as the wine is clear.

Sweet table wines

Up to 200 g of sugar may be added with 2 Campden tablets per 6 bottles of wine after the first racking at the end of fermentation to make a dry table wine into a sweet table wine. Alternatively, saccharin or 100 g of lactose may be used. Always taste the wine first, then sweeten to suit your palate, adding several small doses rather than one large dose. Taste again after each sweetening.

Grape wines

The classical definition of wine is 'the fermented juice of fresh grapes'. It is widely accepted today, however, that wine can be made from innumerable fruits, flowers, vegetables, grains, etc. Grapes are undoubtedly the easiest fruit from which to make wine, and for this reason various ways of making excellent wines from grapes are given first in this section.

8 kg Cypriot seedless grapes, plentifully available during July and August, make 12 bottles of excellent wine. Your greengrocer will let you have a complete tray a little cheaper than the displayed price. Pick the grapes over carefully to remove any green with mould and take out the stalks. Rinse the loose grapes to remove dirt and dust and crush them with your hands, making sure to break each fruit. Pour off the juice, put the pulp into a clean linen cloth and squeeze out the remaining juice. Put the pulp back into a mashing vessel and pour on 3 litres of boiling water, stir, cover and leave for 2 days. About 6 litres of juice will have been extracted from the grapes, and this should be put into a fermentation jar with 2 Campden tablets, and an airlock fitted.

A yeast starter should be prepared with the yeast of your choice, remembering that with care you can impose almost any wine type you choose, for example, burgundy, sauterne, sherry, each make distinctively different wines from these grapes and the result resembles the wine to which the selected yeast is indigenous.

After 2 days' soaking, strain and press the grapes strenuously. It is worth while checking the specific gravity of the pure grapejuice, which experience has shown to vary between 1·050 and 1·080 and of the grape pulp soaked in the water which may have a specific gravity of 1·020 to 1·030. The two musts are now mixed together and sugar is stirred in to bring the specific gravity up to 1·080. The amount will vary from 500 g to 1 kg. The yeast should also be added and the fermentation trap fitted. The jar should be placed in a warm place.

If sherry yeast is being used, the jar should not be filled so full and a good plug of cotton wool used instead of an airlock. As attenuation proceeds, sugar should be added, 100 g at a time, dissolved in some of the wine until the rate of fermentation is so slow that no more can be used. You can try for a dry sherry with a specific gravity of 0·990 or below or an Amontillado type with a specific gravity of 1·000. Remember that the wine will be very high in alcohol – maybe 17 or 18 per cent by volume, and that even with a specific gravity of 1·000 there will be unfermented sugar in the wine. Furthermore, the sherry yeast frequently has a sweetish flavour. Mature this wine for at least a year and longer if possible, racking at least four times.

If a burgundy yeast has been used, the wine should be fermented out to dryness without the addition of any more sugar, and after three rackings may be served cold when it is 1 year old.

If a sauterne yeast has been used the wine should be fermented right out, racked and stored and if necessary sweetened as indicated. The intention is to obtain a wine not too strong in alcohol but with a certain sweetness to make it suitable for serving with fruit salad and ice cream dessert or the like.

English grapes can be used, but they are low in sugar content and high in acid and accordingly they are best used in the making of wine to be fermented by a German wine yeast. The grapes can, of course, also be sweetened with sugar and the acidity diluted with water for use with other yeasts. 8 kg of grapes would need about 1·25 kg sugar and 4 litres of water to make 12 bottles of wine, but hard and fast quantities cannot be given. They depend entirely on the quality of the grapes, which vary from year to year. English grapes and spring vine prunings make excellent additions to any must and improve the vinosity and flavour considerably.

Black grapes, either imported or home grown, can be made into red wine by removing the fruit from the stalks, crushing each berry and leaving the skins in the juice for 2 days. A couple of crushed Campden tablets per 4·5 litres juice should be stirred in and the vessel very well covered. The must should be thoroughly stirred twice a day since the skins float on the surface and tend to dry out. After straining and pressing, the pulp can again be soaked in some boiling water (·5 litre to 1 kg of grapes when whole is a fair proportion), as with the white grapes. Check the gravity with a hydrometer and add sugar only as necessary. All grape wines do well to start at a specific gravity of 1·080 or thereabouts and sugar can be added later for a continued ferment if, for example, you are using a port yeast.

Grapejuice concentrate is very readily available from many suppliers and can be diluted and fermented as required. You can buy the concentrate in 1, 3 and 6 kg containers. 1 kg of concentrate diluted with water makes 6 bottles of table wine.

Yeasts, Nutrients, etc. Yeast starter bottle, liquid yeast, granulated yeast (left-hand spoon). Vierka German yeast (open on left). Respora dried yeast tablets centre. Pectozyme in right-hand spoon, nutrient tablets in front, pH indicator papers back row left

Fermentation jars and locks. The jar on the left contains a fermenting sherry – note size of air space and cotton wool plug. Various locks, all serving the same purpose, are shown

Siphoning. Note the different levels of the jars

Storage vessels. 4-gallon plastic bag, 4-litre bottle in basket, glass storage jar, earthenware storage jar, 5-gallon cask, finished bottle

A great variety of wine types may be bought as well as some interesting fruit and grapejuice blends. Many beginners now start their winemaking with cans of concentrate and move on to country wines after a little experience. The method of fermentation is the same as for other wines. The suppliers often claim that the wine is ready for drinking within 6 weeks, but it is still very young and raw at that time, and needs a proper period of maturation.

Even when well made and matured, wine made from grape-juice concentrate may not be entirely to your satisfaction. There is no doubt, however, that this wine greatly improves other wines, and it is strongly recommended for adding to all country wines, to give them body and vinosity. It can be obtained both red and white, but the quality varies and it is advisable to buy the best.

Flower wines

All flower wines are made in much the same way. The flowers contain no acid and very little tannin and give only bouquet and flavour to the wine. Because they are so sweet smelling, they are not really suitable to serve as 'dry' wines and you will enjoy them best slightly sweet.

Flowers	250 g grapejuice concentrate
1 kg sugar	OR
4 litres water	250 g chopped sultanas
all-purpose yeast and nutrient	15 g acid blend
(this allows the full	½ tsp tannin
bouquet of the flower	3 Campden tablets
to develop)	

Gather the flowers on a warm, sunny day, when the florets are fully open. Remove the petals from the green calices, since the green imparts an unpleasant flavour to the wine.

If fresh flowers are not available you can use a *small* packet of dried flowers from your local herbalist. When flowers are dried their essences become very concentrated.

Pour boiling water on the flowers and when cool add 1 Campden tablet and the acid. Steep the mash for 4 days (closely covered), macerating the petals twice daily, then strain and press out all the essence. Stir in the grapejuice concentrate or chopped sultanas, the sugar, tannin, nutrient and yeast. Ferment in the usual way, removing the sultanas by straining and pressing after 7 days. Continue the fermentation, rack at SG 1·010, add 2 further Campden tablets, then serve as a sweet wine.

Agrimony
1 medium-sized bunch
Carnation
2 litres white 'pinks'
Coltsfoot
2 litres coltsfoot flowers
Dandelion
2 litres dandelion heads
Geranium Leaf
(*Pelargonium quercifolium*)
2 litres of leaves
Hawthorn Blossom
2 litres fresh hawthorn
flowers, pink or white
Primrose
2 litres fresh primroses
Rose Petal
2 litres dark-red petals

Broom
2 litres broom flowers
Clover
2 litres purple clover
Cowslip
2 litres cowslip flowers
Elderflower
1 litre fresh florets
Golden Rod
2 handfuls of blossoms
Marigold
2 litres marigold heads
Oak Leaf
2 litres oak leaves, gathered
when just fully out
Walnut Leaf
1 large handful of walnut
leaves

The measure should be shaken gently but not pressed down.

Fruit, vegetable and other wines

Almond wine

50 g almonds (mostly 'sweet' but include a few 'bitter')
500 g white grapejuice concentrate
OR 500 g chopped sultanas
15 g acid blend
1 kg sugar
4 litres water
sauterne yeast and nutrient

Chop the almonds and sultanas if used, and simmer them for 30 minutes. Strain on to the sugar and stir till it is dissolved. When cool add the acid, nutrient and yeast. Ferment, rack at SG 1·020, add 2 crushed Campden tablets and, when mature, serve sweet.

Apple cider

It is almost impossible to make apple cider without a press. A mixture of different varieties of ripe cider apples must be used and they should be allowed to mellow until they are soft. Wash off dirt and dust, crush the apples thoroughly and press the pulp until it is dry. Add 2 Campden tablets per 4·5 litres of juice. Check the specific gravity with a hydrometer and if needs be add sugar to raise the reading to SG 1·050. Next day add nutrient and all-purpose or champagne yeast, and ferment to dryness. Rack, bottle in beer bottles and prime with not more than 1 tsp sugar per pint bottle. Mature for at least 3 months and serve cool. This cider does not keep for more than 8 or 9 months.

7–9 kg of apples will be needed to make 5 litres of cider.

Apple wine

4–5 kg assorted apples
250 g grapejuice concentrate
OR chopped sultanas
·5–1 kg sugar to give SG 1·084
3 litres water
pectic enzyme
1 Campden tablet
champagne yeast and nutrient

Wash the apples and remove any bad portions, crush them
and add them with the sultanas to 3 litres of water containing
the Campden tablet and some pectic enzyme. Leave in a
warm place for 36 hours. Check the specific gravity and add
sugar as necessary.

Stir in the nutrient and an active yeast and ferment on the
pulp for 5 days, pressing down the fruit cap twice daily.

Strain and press the apples, pour into a fermentation jar, fit
an airlock and ferment out.

Apple will take yeast flavour well, so any variety may be
used. It also blends well with other fruits, e.g. apple and
blackberry, apple and elderberry, etc.

Apple juice

Available in various sized containers.

1·25 litres apple juice
250 g white grapejuice concentrate
750 g white sugar
2·75 litres water
all-purpose yeast and nutrient

Mix all the ingredients together and ferment under an airlock.

Apricot wine

2 kg fresh apricots
250 g grapejuice concentrate
1 kg sugar
3·5 litres water
pectic enzyme
1 Campden tablet
chablis yeast and nutrient

Remove the stones, crush the fruit and drop them into hot water. When cool add the pectic enzyme and Campden tablet. Cover and leave for 36 hours.

Stir in the grapejuice concentrate, nutrient and an active yeast. Ferment on the pulp for 3 days, then strain out the fruit, stir in the sugar, pour into a fermentation jar, fit an air-lock and ferment out.

Apricot (dried) wine

350 g dried apricots
250 g sultanas
1 kg sugar
4 litres water
pectic enzyme
1 Campden tablet
sauterne yeast and nutrient

Wash and chop the apricots and sultanas, place them in a bin and pour boiling water over them. When cool add the pectic enzyme and Campden tablet.

Leave in the warm for 24 hours then stir in the nutrient and yeast. Ferment on the pulp for 3 days.

Strain out the fruit, stir in the sugar, pour into a fermentation jar, fit an airlock and ferment out.

Note These wines are best served slightly sweet, rather than quite dry, so include 100 g of lactose after the first racking or sweeten with saccharin to your taste.

Apricot pulp wine

800 g can apricot pulp
2 kg sugar
pectic enzyme
2 tsp citric acid
1 tsp grape tannin
water to 9 litres
hock yeast and nutrient

Empty the contents of the can into a pan. Fill the can with hot water and empty into the pan. Bring to the boil and simmer for 20 minutes.

Transfer the fruit and juice to a mashing vessel and when cool sprinkle on some pectic enzyme and the citric acid. Cover and leave for 2 days.

Stir in 500 g sugar, the nutrient and the yeast and ferment on the pulp for 2 days, stirring twice daily.

Strain out the pulp through a sieve but do not press it. Stir in the rest of the sugar and make the quantity up to 9 litres with cold water. This makes a pleasant flavoured light dry wine.

A sauterne yeast and 2 litres less water will make a good sweet wine if the fermentation is stopped at SG 1·020.

Artichoke wine

2 kg artichokes
250 g sultanas
1·25 kg sugar
1 lemon and 1 orange
25 g root ginger
½ tsp grape tannin
4 litres water
sherry yeast and nutrient

Scrub the artichokes, thinly peel the orange and lemon, bruise the ginger, chop the sultanas and boil all together for 30 minutes.

Strain when the liquor is cool, stir in the expressed juice of the orange and lemon, the tannin, the nutrient and an active yeast.

Ferment in a jar not quite full and add the sugar in 0·25 kg doses every 7 days.

Banana wine

2 kg very ripe bananas
250 g raisins
1·25 kg sugar
1 lemon and 1 orange
½ tsp grape tannin
4 litres water
all-purpose wine yeast and nutrient
2 Campden tablets

Place the chopped raisins, the peeled and chopped bananas and 4 skins in good condition in a pan, together with the thinly peeled rind of the orange and lemon and boil gently for ½ hour.

When cool strain through a sieve and stir in the sugar, expressed fruit juice, tannin, nutrient and an active yeast. Ferment under an airlock to SG 1·020 then rack and add the Campden tablets to terminate fermentation.

Serve this pleasant, sweet wine cool. The banana, orange and lemon skins improve the flavour – but omit the white pith.

Beetroot wine

2 kg beetroot
250 g raisins
15 g acid blend
15 g root ginger
6 cloves
½ tsp grape tannin
1·5 kg sugar (Demerara or soft brown)
4 litres water
madeira yeast and nutrient

Choose fresh beet of a fair size in the late autumn, scrub them clean, cut them into small dice and boil them until quite tender. When cool strain out the beet but do not press.

Stir in the chopped raisins, acid, tannin, ginger, cloves, nutrient and yeast. Ferment for 5 days, then strain out the solids, pressing the raisins dry.

Stir in brown sugar in ·25 kg doses every 7 days. This will make a very strong wine with the caramel flavour of a madeira wine. Sweeten to taste after racking when fermentation is quite finished.

Birch sap wine

4 litres birch sap
250 g white grapejuice concentrate

1 kg sugar
15 g acid blend
½ tsp grape tannin
all-purpose wine yeast and nutrient

Boil the birch sap gently for 10 minutes to sterilize it. When cool stir in the grapejuice concentrate, sugar, acid, tannin, nutrient and active yeast. Ferment under an airlock to dryness.

Sycamore and walnut sap wine may be made in the same way.

Note Sap should only be taken from mature trees during the first 2 weeks in March when the new sap is rising. Young trees should never be used in case they die.

Bore a hole 1 cm in diameter 35 cm from the ground to a depth just below the bark – about 2 cm.

Push one end of a rubber tube into the hole and the other end into the jar. Plug the neck with cotton wool to keep out insects and cover the jar with a sack to keep out the light. Leave for 2–3 days till the jar is full. Plug the hole in the tree with a piece of well-fitting cork well pushed home.

Blackberry table wine

1·5 kg garden blackberries
250 g chopped raisins
1 kg sugar
4 litres water
pectic enzyme
1 Campden tablet
burgundy yeast and nutrient

Stalk and wash the berries and raisins, crush the berries and pour on boiling water, cover and leave to cool. Add the pectic enzyme and Campden tablet and leave for 24 hours.

Add the nutrient and yeast and ferment on the pulp for 4 days.

Strain out and press the fruit, stir in the sugar, pour into a fermentation jar, fit an airlock and ferment out.

Blackberry dessert wine

2 kg wild blackberries
250 g chopped raisins
1·5 kg sugar
4 litres water
pectic enzyme
1 Campden tablet
port yeast and nutrient

Prepare as for the table wine but continue the fermentation as long as possible by adding only half the sugar at first and the rest in 3 equal doses every 7 days. When fermentation is finished and the wine is racked, sweeten to taste and add the crushed Campden tablet to stabilize the wine during maturation.

Blackcurrant wine

1 kg blackcurrants
500 g dried currants
1·5 kg sugar
4 litres water
pectic enzyme
1 Campden tablet
port yeast and nutrient

Strip, wash and mash the fresh fruit and place it in a bin with the washed and chopped dried fruit. Pour on boiling water and leave to cool. Sprinkle on the pectic enzyme and crushed Campden tablet, cover and leave for 24 hours.

Add the yeast and nutrient and ferment on the pulp for 4 days, pressing down the fruit cap daily.

Strain and press the fruit, stir in half the sugar, pour into a fermentation jar, fit an airlock and ferment for 10 days. Add the remaining sugar in 3 equal doses every 8 days then sweeten to your taste.

Bramble tip wine 1

2 kg young blackberry shoots
250 g white grapejuice concentrate
1 kg sugar
15 g acid blend
$\frac{1}{2}$ tsp grape tannin
4 litres water
hock yeast and nutrient
2 Campden tablets

Wash and cut up the tender shoots and boil them gently for half an hour, strain and when cool stir in the grapejuice concentrate, acid blend, tannin, nutrient and activated hock yeast.

Pour into a fermentation jar, fit an airlock and ferment to SG 1·006.

Rack into a clean jar and add 2 Campden tablets to terminate fermentation.

Bramble tip wine 2

2 kg young blackberry shoots
250 g chopped sultanas
1 kg sugar

10 g of acid blend
½ tsp grape tannin
4 litres water
bordeaux yeast and nutrient

Boil the chopped shoots and sultanas in water for 30 minutes
and leave to cool.

Strain into a bin, add the acid, tannin, sugar, nutrient and
yeast.

Stir well and then pour into a fermentation jar, fit an airlock and ferment to dryness.

Serve cool as a white table wine.

Broad bean wine

2 kg shelled old broad beans
250 g white grapejuice concentrate
1 kg sugar
15 g acid blend
½ tsp grape tannin
4 litres water
hock yeast and nutrient

Boil the beans gently for 1 hour and when cool strain. Stir
in the grapejuice concentrate, sugar, acid, tannin, nutrient
and an active yeast.

Ferment till dry, rack, store and serve cold like a hock.

Bullace wine

2 kg bullaces
250 g chopped raisins
1 kg sugar
4 litres water
pectic enzyme

1 Campden tablet
all-purpose yeast and nutrient

Pour boiling water on to the bullaces and raisins and when cool mash them and remove the stones.

Add the pectic enzyme and Campden tablet, cover and soak for 24 hours.

Stir in the nutrient and yeast and ferment on the pulp for 4 days.

Strain and press the fruit, stir in the sugar, pour into a fermentation jar, fit an airlock and ferment to dryness.

Carrot wine

2 kg good quality carrots
250 g grapejuice concentrate
1 kg sugar
15 g acid blend
½ tsp tannin
4 litres water
all-purpose yeast and nutrient
2 Campden tablets

Scrub and grate the carrots and boil them till tender.

When the liquor is cool strain out the carrots, stir in the grapejuice concentrate, the sugar, acid, tannin, nutrient and an active yeast.

Ferment to SG 1·008 then rack and add crushed Campden tablets to terminate fermentation.

Celery wine

2 kg celery stalks without leaves
250 g white grapejuice concentrate

15 g acid blend
½ tsp grape tannin
1 kg sugar
4 litres water
hock yeast and nutrient
2 Campden tablets

Chop up the celery and boil till tender. Leave to cool, then strain and stir in the grapejuice concentrate, sugar, acid, tannin, nutrient and active yeast.

Pour into a fermentation jar, fit an airlock and ferment to SG 1·006.

Rack and add Campden tablets to terminate fermentation.

Serve cold as a medium sweet wine.

Cherry ale

1 kg Morello cherries
2 litres home-brewed ale
500 g demerara sugar
1 tsp tartaric acid
½ tsp tannin
port yeast and nutrient

Stalk and wash the cherries, remove the stones and place them in a jar with the acid, tannin, nutrient, yeast and sugar dissolved in the beer. Cover with a polythene sheet and secure with a rubber band.

Ferment in a warm place and in due course strain off. When the wine is clear, bottle and store for at least 9 months.

This wine tastes very like cherry brandy. The fruit is delicious in tarts and trifles.

Cherry wine 1 (table)

2 kg mixed cherries (eating and cooking varieties, red and white)
250 g sultanas
1 kg sugar
4 litres water
pectic enzyme
1 Campden tablet
bordeaux yeast and nutrient

Stalk and wash the cherries and sultanas, pour boiling water on to them and when cool mash the fruit and remove the stones.

Add the pectic enzyme and Campden tablet and soak for 24 hours.

Stir in the sugar, nutrient and yeast and ferment on the pulp for 5 days.

Strain and press the fruit and continue fermentation under an airlock.

Cherry wine 2 (sweet)

2 kg Morello cherries
250 g chopped raisins
1·5 kg demerara sugar
4 litres water
pectic enzyme
1 Campden tablet
madeira yeast and nutrient

Prepare as for Cherry Wine 1, but continue fermentation by adding the extra sugar when the specific gravity has fallen to 1·010.

Cherry plum wine

2 kg cherry plums
250 g chopped sultanas
1 kg sugar
2 tsp acid blend
½ tsp tannin
4 litres water
pectic enzyme
3 Campden tablets
sauterne yeast and nutrient

Stalk and wash the fruit, place in a bin and add the chopped sultanas. Pour boiling water over them and when cool mash the fruit with your hands and remove the stones.

Add 1 Campden tablet and the pectic enzyme, cover and leave for 24 hours in a warm place.

Stir in the acid, tannin and sugar, nutrient and active yeast.

Ferment to SG 1·010 then rack and add a further 2 Campden tablets to terminate fermentation.

This makes an excellent all-purpose wine suitable for serving as a dessert wine or as a sweet table wine.

Coffee wine

250 g of Blue Mountain coffee
250 g white grapejuice concentrate
1 kg sugar
15 g acid blend
½ tsp tannin
4 litres water
all-purpose yeast and nutrient
100 g lactose

Simmer the coffee for 20 minutes and leave to cool, then strain on to the sugar and grapejuice concentrate.

Add the acid, tannin, nutrient and an active yeast.

Ferment to dryness, then rack and add the lactose and mature as usual.

This wine is best served medium sweet. It makes an excellent base for a Tia Maria-type liqueur.

Crab-apple wine

2 kg ripe and fleshy crab-apples
250 g chopped sultanas
1 kg sugar
10 g acid blend
4 litres water
pectic enzyme
1 Campden tablet
sauterne yeast and nutrient

Prepare as for Apple Wine.

This wine finishes with a little more body and is best served medium sweet rather than as a dry wine.

Damson wine

2 kg sound ripe damsons
250 g ruby port-type grapejuice concentrate
1·5 kg sugar
2 tsp acid blend
½ tsp grape tannin
4 litres water
pectic enzyme
1 Campden tablet
port yeast and nutrient

Stalk and wash the fruit in very hot water to remove the 'bloom'. Place in a bin and pour boiling water on to them and when cool mash the damsons and remove the stones.

Add the pectic enzyme and Campden tablet, cover and leave for 24 hours in a warm place.

Stir in the grapejuice concentrate, ·5 kg sugar, the acid, tannin, nutrient and an active yeast. Ferment on the pulp for 4 days, then strain and continue fermentation under an airlock in a fermentation jar.

Add 250 g sugar every 8 days from the remainder of the sugar to produce a strong and sweet wine. Mature for 18 months and serve free from chill.

Date wine

2 kg dates
250 g sherry-type grapejuice concentrate
25 g acid blend
$\frac{1}{2}$ tsp tannin
1 kg sugar
4 litres water
sherry yeast and nutrient

Chop and boil the dates gently for half an hour, when cool, strain and stir in the grapejuice concentrate, the acid, tannin, nutrient and yeast.

Ferment as long as possible by adding 250 g of sugar every 8 days and if necessary finish with extra sugar, so that the wine tastes sweet.

Keep for two years and serve this strong sweet wine like a cream sherry.

Elderberry wine 1

Taken from *The Gentleman Gardener* written by the Rev Mr
Stephenson in 1769.

'4½ gallons [20·25 litres] spring water, 1 peck of elderberries
clean picked from their stalks and boil till they begin to dimple.
Strain and to every gallon [4·5 litres] of liquor put 2 lbs [900 g]
Lisbon sugar and boil it 1 hour. Let it cool in a tub not in the
thing that you boil it in for that will make it taste ill. When cool
make a toast of white bread, spread yeast upon it and put it to
the liquor to work for three days, stirring it once or twice every
day, then turn it into a vessel that will just hold it. Add to every
gallon of the liquor 1 lb [450 g] of raisins of the sun and let
them lie in the wine. Bottle in 7 or 8 weeks' time.'

One can imagine that this recipe might very well make a fine
dry wine, though some acid nutrient and a pure yeast and a
fermentation trap would improve the wine considerably.

Elderberry wine 2 (table)

1 kg fresh elderberries, picked clean from their stalks
250 g chopped raisins
1 kg sugar
20 g acid blend
4 litres water
burgundy yeast and nutrient.

Stalk and wash the berries and raisins, mash them with a
wooden spoon and pour boiling water over them. When
cool add the acid, nutrient and yeast.

  Ferment on the pulp for 4 days then strain and press the
fruit.

  Stir in the sugar, pour into a fermentation jar, fit an airlock
and ferment to dryness.

Elderberry wine 3 (sweet)

1 kg fresh elderberries
250 g chopped raisins
250 g dried bananas
1½ kg sugar
20 g acid blend
4 litres water
port yeast and nutrient

Prepare as for elderberry wine 2 but ferment as long as possible, with added sugar if necessary. Keep for 18 months and serve strong and sweet.

Elderberry posset or punch

1 bottle elderberry wine
The rind and juice of a small lemon
6 cloves
1 piece of bruised ginger
1 tbsp honey
2 tbsp sugar

Put all the ingredients into a saucepan, stir steadily, and slowly warm to a temperature of 60°C. This is a delicious drink on a cold night, and is enough for 6 persons.

Fig wine

250 g dried figs
250 g chopped raisins
250 g dried bananas
1 kg brown sugar
15 g acid blend
½ tsp grape tannin

4 litres water
pectic enzyme
1 Campden tablet
tokay yeast and nutrient

Break up the figs, raisins and bananas and pour boiling water over them.

When cool add the acid, pectic enzyme and Campden tablet, cover and leave in the warm for 24 hours.

Next day stir in the nutrient and active yeast and ferment on the pulp for 4 days.

Strain out the fruit, stir in the sugar, pour into a fermentation jar, fit an airlock and ferment as long as possible.

Serve this strong sweet wine at room temperature.

Ginger wine

60 g root ginger
450 g chopped raisins
1 g cayenne pepper
1·25 kg sugar
15 g acid blend
4 litres water
all-purpose yeast and nutrient
2 Campden tablets

Boil all the ingredients except the nutrient and yeast for 20 minutes and leave to cool.

Strain into a fermentation jar, add the nutrient and an active yeast and ferment to SG 1·010.

Rack and add Campden tablets to terminate fermentation. Serve as a sweet wine.

Gooseberry wine 1

1·5 kg hard green gooseberries
250 g white grapejuice concentrate
1 kg sugar
½ tsp grape tannin
4 litres water
pectic enzyme
1 Campden tablet
hock yeast and nutrient

Top, tail and wash the gooseberries, pour boiling water over
them and when cool crush the berries with your hands without breaking the pips. Add Campden tablet and some pectic
enzyme, cover and leave for 24 hours.

Stir in the grapejuice concentrate, tannin, nutrient and an
active yeast.

Ferment on the pulp for 4 days, then strain and press the
fruit, stir in the sugar and continue fermentation to dryness.

Gooseberry wine 2

Ingredients and method as above except that you use only
1 kg gooseberries and a champagne yeast.

When the wine is clear, bottle it in champagne bottles, add
a teaspoonful of sugar, a teaspoonful of active champagne
yeast, fit hollow domed plastic stoppers and wire them down.

Keep the wine for at least 6 months before disgorging the
sediment and serve this attractive wine quite cold.

Note Dessert or very ripe gooseberries are not suitable for
sparkling wine. Use them with a sauterne yeast to make a
sweet wine.

Grapefruit wine

1·25 litre can of grapefruit juice
250 g white grapejuice concentrate
1 kg sugar
3 litres water
chablis yeast and nutrient

Mix all the ingredients together and ferment to dryness.

This makes quite an attractive aperitif type wine.

Hawthorn berry wine

3 litre measure of ripe hawthorn berries
250 g chopped sultanas
1 kg sugar
15 g of acid blend
4 litres water
pectic enzyme
3 Campden tablets
sauterne yeast and nutrient

Pour boiling water over the chopped sultanas and berries and when cool the berries will be soft enough to crush.

Add 1 Campden tablet and the pectic enzyme, together with the acid, and leave for 24 hours.

Stir in the sugar, nutrient and yeast, cover and ferment on the pulp for 4 days, stirring twice daily.

Strain and press the fruit and continue fermentation under an airlock, make a slightly sweet table wine by racking at SG 1·010 and adding a further 2 Campden tablets, crushed, to terminate fermentation.

Lemon wine

8 small lemons
250 g of grapejuice concentrate
1 kg sugar
½ tsp tannin
1 tbsp glycerine
4 litres of water
hock yeast and nutrient

Use only the thinly pared rinds from the lemons and the juice. Avoid all the white pith.

Mix all the ingredients together and ferment for 5 days, remove the lemon skins and continue fermentation.

The glycerine will help to mask the acidity of the lemons.

Lettuce wine

1 kg chopped cos lettuce
4 litres water
500 g chopped sultanas
1 kg sugar
15 g acid blend
½ tsp tannin
hock yeast and nutrient
2 Campden tablets

Clean the lettuce and chop it up, then simmer it for 10 minutes.

Strain on to the chopped sultanas, sugar, acid and tannin.

When cool add the nutrient and yeast, pour the must into a fermentation jar and ferment to SG 1·006.

Then rack and add Campden tablets to terminate fermentation.

Loganberry wine 1 (table)

1 kg ripe loganberries
4 litres water
pectic enzyme
1 Campden tablet
250 g red grapejuice concentrate
bordeaux yeast and nutrient
1 kg sugar

Stalk and wash the loganberries, pour the water over them and when cool add the Campden tablet and pectic enzyme.

Cover and leave for 24 hours then stir in the grapejuice concentrate, the nutrient and the active yeast.

Ferment on the pulp for 4 days, stirring twice daily, then strain and press the fruit, stir in the sugar, pour into a fermentation jar and continue fermentation under an airlock to dryness. This makes an excellent table wine.

Loganberry wine 2 (dessert)

2 kg loganberries
250 g ruby port-type grapejuice concentrate
1·25 kg sugar
4 litres water
pectic enzyme
1 Campden tablet
port yeast and nutrient

Prepare as above, but add the sugar in 250 g doses every 7 days, to continue the fermentation as long as possible.

Finish the wine sweet with some extra sugar to make a strong sweet wine.

Maize wine

500 g crushed maize
1 kg chopped raisins
1 kg sugar
4 litres water
10 g acid blend
½ tsp tannin
cereal yeast and nutrient

Mince the maize to crush it, add the chopped raisins, acid, tannin and sugar. Pour on the boiling water and stir well. When cool add the nutrient and yeast.

Ferment on the pulp for 4 days, stirring twice daily, then strain out the solids and continue fermentation under an airlock.

Mangold wine

2 kg mangolds
500 g chopped sultanas
1 kg sugar
4 litres water
½ tsp grape tannin
15 g acid blend
all-purpose yeast and nutrient

Scrub and dice the mangolds, boil with the sugar and acid until they are tender. Strain on to the chopped sultanas and when cool add the tannin, nutrient and yeast.

Ferment for 7 days, stirring daily, then strain out the sultanas and continue fermentation under an airlock.

This wine may be served dry as a table wine or sweetened slightly for social purposes.

Marrow wine

2 kg ripe marrow
250 g chopped sultanas
1 kg sugar
15 g acid blend
½ tsp tannin
25 g crushed root ginger
4 litres water
all-purpose yeast and nutrient

Wipe the marrow clean and grate it coarsely into a mashing vessel. Include the skin and seeds, the bruised ginger and the chopped sultanas, together with the acid, tannin and sugar.

Pour boiling water over them and stir well. When cool, add the nutrient and yeast, ferment on the pulp for 4 days, stirring twice daily, strain out and press the solids and continue fermentation under an airlock.

You may prefer this wine not quite dry.

Medlar wine

2 kg medlars
500 g sultanas
1 kg sugar
2 tsp tartaric acid
½ tsp tannin
4 litres water
pectic enzyme
1 Campden tablet
sauterne yeast and nutrient

Use only fully ripe and soft medlars.

Wash and crush them, add the chopped sultanas, pour on

boiling water and when cool add Campden tablet and the pectic enzyme, acid and tannin.

Cover and steep for 24 hours, then stir in the sugar, nutrient and yeast and ferment on the pulp for 5 days. Strain out the fruit and continue fermentation under an airlock.

Mixed fruit wine 1 (table)

1·5 kg mixed fruit (black, white and red currants, raspberries, strawberries, cherries, plums, etc., etc.)
250 g grapejuice concentrate
1 kg sugar
4 litres water
pectic enzyme
1 Campden tablet
bordeaux yeast and nutrient

Wash clean and mash the fruit and pour on boiling water. When cool add Campden tablet and the pectic enzyme.

Next day stir in the grapejuice concentrate, nutrient and yeast. Ferment for 4 days pressing down the fruit cap twice daily.

Strain and press the fruit and continue fermentation under an airlock.

Mixed fruit wine 2 (dessert)

2 kg mixed fruit as above
250 g ruby port-type grapejuice concentrate
1·5 g sugar
pectic enzyme
1 Campden tablet
4 litres water
port yeast and nutrient

Make the wine in the same way as above but continue the fermentation to produce a dessert wine by adding the sugar in 250 g doses every 7 days.

Finish the wine sweet.

Mixed dried fruit wine 1 (table)

1 kg mixed dried fruit (sultanas, currants, raisins)
500 g sugar
10 g acid blend
½ tsp tannin
4 litres water
bordeaux yeast and nutrient

Chop up the dried fruit and place it in a bin. Pour on the boiling water and when cool stir in the acid, tannin, nutrient and an active yeast.

Ferment on the pulp for 7 days, pressing down the fruit cap daily.

Strain out the fruit and press it dry then stir in the sugar and continue the fermentation under an airlock.

This makes a fine dry table wine.

Mixed dried fruit wine 2 (dessert)

Ingredients as above but use a sherry yeast and continue fermentation as long as possible by the addition of the sugar in 250 g doses every 7 or 8 days.

Finish the wine sweet. (250 g dried bananas chopped up with the other dried fruit improves the body of this wine and helps to create a rich dessert 'sherry-type' wine.)

Mulberry wine 1 (table)

1 kg mulberries
250 g red grapejuice concentrate

1 kg sugar
4 litres water
½ tsp tannin
pectic enzyme
1 Campden tablet
burgundy yeast and nutrient

Stalk and wash the mulberries, pour on the boiling water and when cool add Campden tablet and the pectic enzyme. Cover and soak for 24 hours.

Stir in the grapejuice concentrate, tannin and the nutrient and ferment on the pulp for 4 days.

Strain and press the fruit, stir in the sugar and continue the fermentation under an airlock. This makes an excellent table wine.

Mulberry wine 2 (sweet)

1·5 kg mulberries
250 g chopped raisins
1·15 kg brown sugar
4 litres water
pectic enzyme
1 Campden tablet
½ tsp grape tannin
madeira yeast and nutrient

Prepare this wine as for a table wine but add only half the sugar in the first instance and add the remaining sugar in 250 g doses every 8 days to prolong the fermentation to as high a degree of alcohol formation as possible.

Finish the wine sweet.

Orange wine 1

1·25 litre can orange juice
250 g white grapejuice concentrate
500 g sugar
3 litres water
sauterne yeast and nutrient

Mix all the ingredients together and ferment to dryness under an airlock. When fermentation is finished, sweeten the wine to taste with a little saccharin or lactose.

Orange wine 2 (aperitif)

5 Seville oranges
5 sweet oranges
5 ripe bananas
250 g white grapejuice concentrate
1·5 kg sugar
4 litres water
sherry yeast and nutrient

Thinly peel three Sevilles and two sweet oranges and put the peeled and mashed bananas into a bin. Pour on hot water and when cool add all the orange juice, the grapejuice concentrate, the nutrient and an active yeast.

Ferment for 4 days, then strain out the peel, add 500 g sugar and continue the fermentation for as long as possible by adding 250 g every 7 days.

Finish this strong wine not quite dry and, when it is well matured, serve it cool as a splendid aperitif.

Parsley wine

500 g fresh parsley leaves (best picked in June before the flavour becomes too strong)
250 g white grapejuice concentrate
1 kg sugar
10 g acid blend
½ tsp grape tannin
4 litres water
chablis yeast and nutrient

Boil the parsley for 20 minutes and leave to cool, strain and stir in all the other ingredients and ferment to dryness under an airlock. This makes a delicious table wine with fish dishes.

A hock yeast may be used as an alternative, and 1 packet of dried parsley from a herbalist may be used instead of the fresh parsley. It should be soaked in water for 24 hours before boiling.

Parsnip wine

2 kg prepared parsnips
250 g white grapejuice concentrate
2 kg sugar
10 g acid blend
½ tsp tannin
4 litres water
sauterne yeast and nutrient
2 Campden tablets

The parsnips should be well frosted, and the best time to make this wine is about the end of January.

Scrub and dice the parsnips, removing any bad or rusty

portions. Boil the parsnip pieces until they are just tender but not squashy.

When cool strain on to all the other ingredients and ferment to SG 1·010, then rack and add crushed Campden tablets to terminate fermentation.

Peach wine 1

1·25 kg ripe peaches
250 g sauterne-type grapejuice concentrate
1 kg sugar
10 g tartaric acid
½ tsp tannin
3·5 litres water
pectic enzyme
3 Campden tablets
sauterne yeast and nutrient

Split the peaches to remove the stones, pour on the boiling water and when cool mash the now soft fruit with your hands.

Add the acid, tannin, 1 Campden tablet and pectic enzyme, cover and soak for 24 hours.

Stir in the grapejuice concentrate, nutrient and an active yeast. Ferment on the pulp for 4 days, pressing down the cap twice daily.

Strain out the fruit rolling it round a sieve rather than pressing it. Stir in the sugar and continue fermentation to SG 1·010.

Rack and add a further 2 Campden tablets to terminate fermentation, so that the wine tastes sweet.

Peach wine 2 (dessert)

1·5 kg peaches
250 g white grapejuice concentrate

1·5 kg sugar
3·5 litres water
10 g tartaric acid
½ tsp tannin
pectic enzyme
1 Campden tablet
tokay yeast and nutrient

Prepare as above but continue fermentation by adding the sugar in 250 g doses. Finish the wine sweet and serve it as a strong dessert wine.

Peach pulp wine

1 A2½ size can peach pulp
500 g grapejuice concentrate
2 kg sugar
25 g acid blend
1 tsp grape tannin
water to 4·5 litres
pectic enzyme
2 Campden tablets
all-purpose yeast and nutrient

Empty the contents of the can into a saucepan, fill the can with hot water and pour that in too.

Boil the pulp till tender, add another 4 litres cold water, transfer the fruit and juice to a mashing vessel. When it cools sprinkle on the pectic enzyme and the acid. Cover and leave for 2 days in a warm place.

Stir in the grapejuice concentrate, the nutrient and a fermenting yeast, cover and leave for 2 more days, pressing down the cap twice daily.

Strain and roll the pulp in a sieve, stir in the rest of the sugar and with cold boiled water make up to 7 litres for a sweet wine and 9 litres for a dry wine.

Continue fermentation to SG 1·016 for a sweet wine, then rack and add Campden tablets or ferment out for a dry wine.

Pea-pod wine

2 kg fresh young pea-pods
250 g white grapejuice concentrate
1 kg sugar
15 g acid blend
½ tsp tannin
4 litres water
hock yeast and nutrient

Boil the pods till tender and when cool strain on to all the other ingredients. Stir well and ferment under an airlock to dryness.

This makes a light table wine.

Pear wine

2 kg hard cooking pears
250 g white grapejuice concentrate
1 kg sugar
10 g acid blend
4 litres water
pectic enzyme
1 Campden tablet
champagne yeast and nutrient

Cut up the pears and drop them into cold water containing the acid and the Campden tablet.

Add the pectic enzyme and cover and soak for 24 hours.

Add the grapejuice concentrate, the nutrient and an active

champagne yeast and ferment on the pulp for 4 days, pressing down the cap daily.

Strain and press the fruit, stir in the sugar and continue fermentation to dryness. Rack and store in the usual way.

If you wish to make a sparkling wine, rack into champagne bottles after 6 months and add a level teaspoonful of sugar to each bottle together with a teaspoonful of an actively fermenting champagne yeast from a starter bottle.

Fit hollow domed plastic stoppers and wire them down. Mature for at least a further 6 months before disgorging the sediment from the secondary fermentation.

Pineapple wine

4 fresh pineapples
250 g white grapejuice concentrate
1 kg sugar
10 g acid blend
4 litres water
all-purpose yeast and nutrient

Top and tail the fresh pineapples, chop them up and boil them gently in 2 litres of water for 15 minutes. When cool strain and stir in all the other ingredients. Ferment under an airlock to dryness.

This wine makes an excellent aperitif. It can also be sweetened and served as a table wine.

Potato wine

2 kg old potatoes
250 g white grapejuice concentrate
1·5 kg sugar
4 litres water
1 large piece root ginger

rind and juice of 1 large lemon
1 bitter orange
cereal yeast and nutrient

Scrub the potatoes clean, but do not peel them. Cut them into
1·25 cm cubes and boil them with the ginger and fruit peel till
tender.

When cool strain on to the other ingredients and ferment
under an airlock.

Finish the wine sweet and keep it until it is well matured.

Plum wine (bush plum)

2 kg small red/black plums
250 g red grapejuice concentrate
1 kg sugar
4 litres water
pectic enzyme
1 Campden tablet
bordeaux yeast and nutrient

Wash the fruit thoroughly in hot water to remove the waxy
'bloom' then stone and crush the fruit, pour on boiling water,
cover and leave to cool.

Add 1 Campden tablet and the pectic enzyme, leave for
24 hours.

Next day stir in the grapejuice concentrate, the nutrient and
active yeast. Ferment on the pulp for 4 days, pressing down the
cap each day.

Strain and press the fruit, add the sugar and ferment under
an airlock. This makes a very good dry table wine for everyday drinking.

Plum wine (victoria)

2 kg plums
250 g white grapejuice concentrate
1·5 kg sugar
1½ tsp tartaric acid
½ tsp grape tannin
3·5 litres water
pectic enzyme
1 Campden tablet
sherry yeast and nutrient

Thoroughly wash the fruit in hot water to remove the waxy 'bloom'. Stone and crush the fruit, pour on boiling water and when cool add Campden tablet, the pectic enzyme, the acid and tannin.

Leave for 24 hours then stir in the grapejuice concentrate, nutrient and an active yeast.

Ferment on the pulp for 4 days, pressing down the pulp each day.

Strain out and press the fruit and stir in half the sugar. Continue fermentation under an airlock.

Add the remaining sugar in 4 doses at 8-day intervals.

Finish this wine strong and dry, mature well and serve it cool as an aperitif.

Prune wine

1 kg prunes
500 g raisins
1·5 kg brown sugar
15 g acid blend
½ tsp grape tannin

4 litres water
madeira yeast and nutrient

Wash the prunes and raisins quickly in hot water and place them in a bin and pour on boiling water.

When cool, break up the fruit and remove the stones, add the acid, tannin, nutrient and yeast and ferment on the pulp for 4 days.

Strain out the fruit and stir in ·5 kg sugar and ferment under an airlock.

Add the remaining sugar in 4 equal doses every 8 days to make a strong sweet wine.

Quince wine

2 kg ripe quinces
250 g grapejuice concentrate
1 kg sugar
2 tsp tartaric acid
½ tsp tannin
4 litres water
pectic enzyme
3 Campden tablets
all-purpose yeast and nutrient

Wash and crush or grate the quinces, omitting the cores, and drop them into hot water. When cool add 1 Campden tablet and the pectic enzyme, the acid and tannin. Next day, stir in the grapejuice concentrate, the nutrient and an active yeast and ferment on the pulp for 4 days.

Strain and press the fruit, stir in the sugar and continue fermentation to SG 1·006, then rack and add a further 2 Campden tablets, crushed, to terminate fermentation.

Serve as a medium sweet wine. The flavour is impaired if the wine is too sweet and less pleasant if wholly dry.

Raisin wine 1 (table)

2 kg chopped raisins
2 tsp acid blend
$\frac{1}{2}$ tsp grape tannin
4 litres water
pectic enzyme
3 Campden tablets
sauterne yeast and nutrient

Wash and chop the raisins, pour on the boiling water, cover and when cool add the acid, tannin, pectic enzyme and 1 Campden tablet. Cover and leave till next day.

Stir in the nutrient and an active yeast and ferment on the pulp for 7 days, pressing down the cap each day.

Strain and press the raisins, then continue fermentation to SG 1·010.

Rack and add 2 further Campden tablets, crushed, to terminate fermentation so that this wine may be served as a medium sweet table wine.

Raisin wine 2 (dessert)

2 kg best large raisins
500 g demerara sugar
4 litres water
2 tsp acid blend
$\frac{1}{2}$ tsp grape tannin
pectic enzyme
1 Campden tablet
madeira yeast and nutrient

Prepare as for the previous recipe but omit the final 2 Campden tablets and add the sugar in 5 doses of 100 g every 4 days.

Ferment in a very warm place and finish as a strong, sweet wine.

It will be found, when well matured, that this wine has a pleasant caramellized flavour reminiscent of madeira wine.

Raspberry wine

1 kg ripe raspberries
250 g red grapejuice concentrate
1 kg sugar
4 litres water
pectic enzyme
1 Campden tablet
burgundy yeast and nutrient

Stalk, wash and crush the raspberries and pour cold water on to them. Add Campden tablet and the pectic enzyme, cover and leave till next day.

Stir in the grapejuice concentrate, nutrient and the active yeast and ferment on the pulp for 4 days.

Strain out the fruit, rolling it round a sieve rather than pressing it, stir in the sugar and continue fermentation under an airlock till SG 1·006.

The flavour of this wine is very pungent and it does not make a good dry wine but is best served slightly sweet.

Redcurrant wine

1 kg redcurrants
250 g white grapejuice concentrate
1 kg sugar
2 tsp glycerine
4 litres water

pectic enzyme
2 Campden tablets
bordeaux yeast and nutrient

Strip, wash, drain and mash the currants, pour cold water on to them, add 1 Campden tablet and the pectic enzyme. Cover and leave for 24 hours.

Stir in the grapejuice concentrate, the nutrient and the active yeast.

Ferment for 4 days on the pulp, pressing down the cap daily.

Strain out the fruit, rolling it round a sieve, stir in the sugar and continue fermentation under an airlock.

Rack, add the glycerine and a further Campden tablet.

This makes an excellent rosé table wine. The glycerine masks the high acidity of the redcurrants.

Rhubarb wine (table)

2 kg ripe red-skinned rhubarb gathered in late May or early June
250 g white grapejuice concentrate
the rind only of a large lemon
1 kg sugar
½ tsp tannin
4 litres water
pectic enzyme
1 Campden tablet
hock yeast and nutrient

Trim off the leaf and about 2 cm stalk. Cut off the white foot from the root end of the rhubarb. Wipe the stalks clean and chop them small, add the thinly pared lemon rind but no juice.

Pour boiling water over the fruit and when it is cool, crush the now soft rhubarb with your hands. Add the pectic enzyme and Campden tablet, leave for 24 hours then stir in the grapejuice concentrate, the nutrient and an active yeast.

Ferment on the pulp for 4 days, then strain out the fruit, stir in the sugar and continue the fermentation under an air-lock.

This makes a light table wine that is often ready for drinking within 9 months.

Rhubarb wine (sweet)

Ingredients and method as above but increase the grapejuice concentrate to 500 g and use a sauterne yeast.

Rack at SG 1·010 and add 2 crushed Campden tablets to terminate fermentation. This makes a sweet table wine, suitable for the dessert course of a meal.

Rice and raisin wine

500 g flaked rice
500 g chopped raisins
1 kg sugar
the rind and juice of 1 large lemon
4 litres water
sherry yeast and nutrient

Pour boiling water on to the rice, raisins, sugar and lemon rind. Stir well to dissolve the sugar and when cool, add the lemon juice, nutrient and an active yeast.

Ferment for a week, stirring daily, then strain and continue the fermentation to the end.

When fermentation is over, rack into a clean jar and rack as often as is necessary to reduce the sediment and thereby improve the flavour.

The wine is best finished slightly sweet, since it has a full body.

Rosehip wine (table)

3 litre measure of fresh ripe rosehips
250 g sultanas
1 kg sugar
rind and juice of 1 large lemon
4 litres water
pectic enzyme
3 Campden tablets
sauterne yeast and nutrient

Wash and crush the berries and sultanas, pour boiling water on to them and when cool add the rind and juice of the lemon, 1 Campden tablet and the pectic enzyme.

Cover and leave for 24 hours then stir in the sugar, nutrient and yeast.

Ferment for 5 days, then strain and continue the fermentation under an airlock.

Terminate fermentation at SG 1·010 by racking into a clean jar and adding 2 more Campden tablets.

Rosehip wine (dessert)

Ingredients and method as above except that you use 1·5 kg sugar, 500 g sultanas and a sherry yeast. Continue the fermentation by omitting the last 2 Campden tablets, and by adding the sugar in small doses to produce a strong sweet dessert type wine.

Rosehip and fig wine

250 g dried rosehip shells
200 g chopped figs
250 g white grapejuice concentrate
1·5 kg sugar

15 g acid blend
½ tsp tannin
4 litres water
pectic enzyme
1 Campden tablet
tokay yeast and nutrient

Pour boiling water on to the rosehip shells and chopped figs and when cool add Campden tablet and the pectic enzyme, the acid and the tannin. Cover and leave for 24 hours.

Next day stir in the grapejuice concentrate, the nutrient and an active yeast.

Ferment on the pulp for 4 or 5 days, then strain out the fruit, stir in half the sugar and continue fermentation under an airlock. Add the remaining sugar in small doses to produce a strong, sweet wine.

This excellent dessert wine should be matured for at least 18 months. Do not use more figs, because of their strong flavour.

Rose petal wine

1 litre strongly scented dark red rose petals
4 litres water
500 g grapejuice concentrate
1 kg sugar
15 g acid blend
½ tsp tannin
all-purpose yeast and nutrient
2 Campden tablets

Pour boiling water on to the rose petals and macerate them with a wooden spoon, cover and soak for 2 days, macerating the petals twice each day.

Strain and press the petals, stir in all the other ingredients except the Campden tablets and ferment to SG 1·016.

Rack into a clean jar, add crushed Campden tablets to terminate fermentation, so that the wine may be served sweet.

White grapejuice concentrate makes a pretty rosé-type wine, red grapejuice concentrate makes a well flavoured red social wine.

Rowanberry wine

1 kg ripe rowanberries
250 g crushed wheat
250 g chopped sultanas
1 kg sugar
25 g bruised root ginger
15 g acid blend
4 litres water
all-purpose yeast and nutrient

Pour boiling water on to the stalked and washed berries, wheat, sultanas and ginger. When cool add all the other ingredients and ferment on the pulp for 3 days, then strain, press and continue fermentation under an airlock.

The rowanberry is rather bitter and too many berries should therefore not be used. It is better to serve this wine sweet rather than dry.

Sloe wine (table)

1·5 kg ripe sloes
250 g red grapejuice concentrate
2 tsp tartaric acid
½ tsp tannin
1 kg sugar
4 litres water

pectic enzyme
1 Campden tablet
bordeaux yeast and nutrient

Stalk and wash the sloes. Pour boiling water on to them and when cool crush the now soft berries with your hands.

Add Campden tablet, the acid, tannin and pectic enzyme. Cover and leave for 24 hours.

Next day add the grapejuice concentrate, nutrient and active yeast and ferment on the pulp for 4 days. Strain and press. Stir in the sugar and ferment to dryness under an airlock.

This makes an attractive dry table wine that may be served with steak, chops or cheese.

Sloe wine (dessert)

Make in the same way as for the previous recipe but add 250 g chopped dried bananas to the sloes. Use a port yeast and another 400 g of sugar during fermentation added in 4 × 100 g doses at 7-day intervals.

This produces a sweet dessert wine.

Spinach wine

1 kg spinach
500 g white grapejuice concentrate
1 kg sugar
2 tsp tartaric acid
4 litres water
all-purpose yeast and nutrient

Wash, chop and boil the spinach till cooked. When cool, strain on to all the other ingredients and ferment under an airlock.

Strong wine or 'poor man's brandy'

500 g crushed wheat
1 kg old potatoes
1 kg chopped raisins
1 kg demerara sugar
rind and juice of 2 large lemons
2 tsp tartaric acid
½ tsp tannin
4 litres water
cereal yeast and nutrient

Scrub the potatoes and cut them small. Wash the wheat and raisins, thinly pare the lemons and put all these ingredients into a mashing vessel. Pour boiling water on to them and leave to cool. Stir in the acid, tannin, nutrient, active yeast, and ferment on the pulp for 4 days.

Strain out all the solids and continue the fermentation, adding the sugar in 4 equal doses at 8-day intervals.

Finish the wine sweet at SG 1·020 then rack and mature for at least 2 years.

Sugar-beet wine

2 kg sugar-beet
25 g bruised root ginger
250 g of chopped sultanas
1 kg sugar
rind and juice of 2 large lemons
4 litres of water
2 Campden tablets
all-purpose yeast and nutrient

Scrub and dice the sugar-beet and simmer with the ginger for

1½ hours. When cool strain on to the chopped sultanas, add the lemon juice, sugar, nutrient and an active yeast.

Ferment under an airlock, but terminate fermentation at SG 1·010 by racking into a clean jar and adding 2 crushed Campden tablets.

Sultana wine

2 kg chopped sultanas
250 g dried bananas
rind and juice of a large lemon
500 g sugar
4 litres water
pectic enzyme
1 Campden tablet
sherry yeast and nutrient

Pour boiling water on to the chopped sultanas, bananas and thinly pared lemon rind. When cool add pectic enzyme and Campden tablet. Next day stir in the lemon juice, nutrient and an active yeast.

Ferment on the pulp for 4 days, pressing down the cap daily.

Strain and press the pulp and continue fermentation for as long as possible by adding the sugar in 4 equal doses at 8-day intervals.

The wine may be sweet or dry, as you wish, but should be racked several times during maturation.

Tea wine

4 litres cold tea
500 g chopped raisins
1 kg sugar

rind and juice of an orange and a lemon
all-purpose yeast and nutrient

The tea may be saved from several pots or be freshly made.

Chop up the raisins, add to the tea with the thinly pared rind and juice of the orange and lemon.

Stir in the nutrient and an active yeast.

Ferment for 7 days, then strain and press, stir in the sugar and continue fermentation.

You may finish this wine either sweet or dry as you prefer, but experience shows that it is often preferred slightly sweet.

Vine prunings wine

2 kg vine prunings
250 g sultanas
1 kg sugar
4 litres water
2 tsp tartaric acid
½ tsp tannin
hock yeast and nutrient

Wash the prunings in clean cold water, chop them up into small pieces and place them in a bin with the chopped sultanas.

Pour boiling water on to them and when cool, add the acid, tannin, nutrient and an active yeast.

Ferment on the pulp for 5 days then strain and press the solids, stir in the sugar and continue fermentation to dryness.

Note The vine leaves and tendrils should be taken from a vine or vines which have not been sprayed with Bordeaux mixture i.e. copper-sulphate solution.

Wheat and raisin wine

500 g crushed wheat
500 g chopped raisins
1 kg sugar
4 litres water
10 g acid blend
½ tsp tannin
cereal yeast and nutrient

Wash the wheat and then crush it in the mincer. Chop the dried fruit, add the acid, tannin and sugar and pour on boiling water. Stir well, cover and leave till cool.

Add the nutrient and active yeast. Ferment for a week, pressing down the cap daily.

Strain and continue the fermentation, then rack and mature.

Whortleberry wine 1 (table)

1 kg whortleberries
250 g red grapejuice concentrate
1 kg sugar
4 litres water
pectic enzyme
1 Campden tablet
bordeaux yeast and nutrient

Wash the fruit and pour boiling water on to it. When cool, crush it with your hands, add Campden tablet and the pectic enzyme, cover and leave for 1 day.

Stir in the grapejuice concentrate, nutrient and an active yeast.

Ferment on the pulp for 4 days then strain out the fruit, stir in the sugar and continue fermentation under an airlock to dryness. This makes a splendid red table wine.

Whortleberry wine 2 (dessert)

1·5 kg whortleberries
250 g red grapejuice concentrate
1·25 kg sugar
4 litres water
pectic enzyme
1 Campden tablet
port yeast and nutrient

Prepare as above but continue fermentation as long as possible, adding additional sugar in small doses.

Finish the wine sweet.

Whortleberry wine 3

350 g dried whortleberries
250 g raisins
10 g acid blend
$\frac{1}{2}$ tsp tannin
1·25 kg sugar
4 litres water
pectic enzyme
1 Campden tablet
port yeast and nutrient

Wash the berries free from dust and preservative, place them in a bin with the chopped raisins and pour boiling water over them.

When cool add the pectic enzyme, acid, tannin and Campden tablet.

Next day, add the nutrient and active yeast and ferment on the pulp for 4 days, pressing down the cap daily.

Strain and stir in the sugar, and ferment out. Finish the wine slightly sweet.

Note Sometimes the whortleberry is called the bilberry and in other places the blueberry. It is, however, the same fruit by whatever name it is called.

Appendix 1 Table of specific gravity, sugar and alcohol content

specific gravity	sugar in 4·54 litres kg	sugar in 5 litres kg	% alcohol
1·005	0·057	0·063	0·71
1·010	0·113	0·125	1·39
1·015	0·170	0·188	2·05
1·020	0·227	0·250	2·71
1·025	0·284	0·313	3·42
1·030	0·340	0·375	4·08
1·035	0·397	0·438	4·75
1·040	0·453	0·500	5·44
1·045	0·510	0·563	6·13
1·050	0·568	0·625	6·99
1·055	0·624	0·688	7·47
1·060	0·681	0·750	8·18
1·065	0·724	0·797	8·84
1·070	0·780	0·859	9·53
1·075	0·823	0·906	10·19
1·080	0·880	0·969	10·89
1·085	0·936	1·031	11·61
1·090	0·993	1·094	12·31
1·095	1·036	1·140	12·92
1·100	1·078	1·188	13·54
1·105	1·135	1·250	14·24
1·110	1·192	1·313	14·98
1·115	1·234	1·359	15·62
1·120	1·277	1·406	16·32
1·125	1·334	1·469	17·01

Figures correct at 20°C.
At 25°C add 2 to the specific gravity reading

30°C	3½
35°C	5

Appendix 2 Metric conversion tables

Solids

1 g	= 0·035	oz
10 g	= 0·35	oz
25 g	= 0·825	oz
50 g	= 1·75	oz
100 g	= 3·5	oz
454 g	= 1·0	lb
1 kg	= 2·20	lb

Liquids

5 ml	= 1	teaspoonful
0·25 litre	= $8\frac{3}{4}$	fl oz
0·5 litre	= $17\frac{1}{2}$	fl oz
0·75 litre	= $26\frac{2}{3}$	fl oz
1 litre	= $1\frac{3}{4}$	pints
4·5 litre	= 1	gallon
5 litre	= $8\frac{3}{4}$	pints

Note

8 pints = 10 USA pints

Temperature

0°C =	32°F
10°C =	50°F
15°C =	59°F
20°C =	68°F
25°C =	77°F
60°C =	140°F
65°C =	149°F
100°C =	212°F

Proof spirit

14% alcohol =	25° proof
29% alcohol =	50° proof
40% alcohol =	70° proof
50% alcohol =	87° proof
80% alcohol =	140° proof

Appendix 3 **Some major suppliers**

March 1976)

1 Grape juice and malt extract concentrates

Boots the Chemist Nottingham
C.W.E. The Winery, Cawston, Norwich
Edme Mistley, Manningtree, Essex
Hidalgo 81 Ledbury Rd, London, W11
Itona Leyland Mill Lane, Wigan
Tom Caxton Carrow, Norwich
Solvino 678 High Rd, Finchley, London N12
Southern Vineyards Hove, Sussex
Unican Central Trading Estate, Bath Rd, Bristol, BS4 3EH

2 Yeast

C.W.E. See above
Leigh Williams Tattenhall, Cheshire
Unican See above

3 Equipment and Ingredients by

Mail Order
Loftus 16 The Terrace, Torquay
Ritchie 60 Victoria St, Burton-on-Trent
Vina St John's Rd, Liverpool
Winecraft Slate St, Leicester
Retail shops
Boots the Chemist most Branches
Home Brew Shops most towns
Loftus Charlotte St, London NW1

4 Journals

Amateur Winemaker South St, Andover, Hants
Home Beer and Winemaking PO Box No 1, Wirral, Merseyside

Index

H. E. Bravery
**The Complete Book of
Home Winemaking** 75p

'Many people still imagine that all home-made wines are makeshift,
inferior products . . . the truth is that well-made home-made wine,
made with a good recipe and method and a bit of commonsense, is
as good and often better than commercial products' — from the
author's introduction.

The recipes are new and economical, but thoroughly tried and
tested ; the methods are simply explained and easy to follow.

Edmund Penning-Rowsell
Red, White and Rosé 60p

A complete guide for the beginner to the fascinating subject of
wines, by a recognized authority, the Wine Correspondent for
Country Life and the *Financial Times*.

Red, White and Rosé gives full information on wines of the world ;
the wines of France, Germany, Italy, Portugal and Spain and other
European countries ; also those of Australia, South Africa and the
USA. There is advice on how to choose, serve and enjoy wines.
This is not only a concise course of instruction but a remarkable
reference book you will always want to have at your fingertips.

Katie Stewart
The Times Cookery Book £1.50

Carefully chosen from the recipes published in *The Times* over the
last few years, and including many new ones, this collection of
recipes by Katie Stewart is practical, varied and imaginative.

Selected to suit both everyday needs and special occasions, these
recipes provide a rich source of new ideas for anyone who enjoys
cooking.

Brian G. Furner
The Kitchen Garden 60p

A comprehensive guide to providing your family with healthy, nourishing food all the year round.

Here is sound, practical advice by a well-known vegetable specialist – on planning your garden space; how to dig; fertilizing the soil; what to sow. There is a monthly time-table of essential jobs, and many labour-saving hints are given.

'Splendid value' HOME GARDENER

Dorothy Hall
The Book of Herbs 70p

The unique flavours, perfumes, oil and mineral supplies and antiseptic properties of herbs have for centuries made them indispensable as aids to health and well-being.

In this complete and thorough guide, Dorothy Hall shows how to grow herbs and how to use them in cooking, for beauty and health, to control garden pests – and even as snuff and tobacco.

The author's approach to health foods and medicines, to conservation and ecology, makes this a reliable guide to herbs and their natural and non-polluting uses.

You can buy these and other Pan Books from booksellers and newsagents; or direct from the following address:
Pan Books, Sales Office, Cavaye Place, London SW10 9PG
Send purchase price plus 20p for the first book and 10p for each additional book, to allow for postage and packing
Prices quoted are applicable in the UK

While every effort is made to keep prices low, it is sometimes necessary to increase prices at short notice. Pan Books reserve the right to show on covers and charge new retail prices which may differ from those advertised in the text or elsewhere.